David
Sutherland

D1088871

On Wilderness Trails

On Wilderness Trails

W. Phillip Keller

Photographs by the author

Line drawings by Geraldine Locke

Baker Book House
Grand Rapids, Michigan 49506

These chapters were selected from CANADA'S WILD GLORY © 1961 by W. Phillip
Keller and are used with permission of the copyright owner. All photographs were taken
by the author and are his exclusive copyright. Printed in the United States of America.
First printing, July 1980
ISBN: 0-8010-5421-4

To
MY WILD FRIENDS
of
HOOF, WING, AND CLAW

I will lift up mine eyes
unto the hills,
from whence cometh my help.
My help cometh from the Lord,
which made heaven and earth.
Psalm 121:1, 2

In Appreciation

Most of my wilderness wanderings have been solitary journeys. Yet here and there along the side roads and pack trails of Canada friends have been made who added great zest to my 'back-country' days.

I mention especially the game wardens, the park officials, the wildlife biologists, and the forest rangers. Some of these men have not only shared their own intimate knowledge of the wilds with me, but also their bunks, bread, and vehicles.

For their never-failing interest and encouragement I am especially grateful to Dr. C. Carl of the British Columbia Provincial Museum in Victoria, and to Inspector Stevenson, now retired from the B.C. Game Department.

Most deserving of all is my family, whose unbounded enthusiasm is a contagious delight.

For the superb sketches I am indebted to Geraldine Locke, who rescued me so graciously from the ignominious fate of having to use my own crude drawings.

In preparing some of the photographs Mr. John Gerald of Munshaws in Vancouver gave me generous assistance.

On Wilderness Trails

With a heave a ho, I shoulder my pack.
I'm anxious to go, away up and back.
With light heart and free, my footsteps are brisk,
For up there you see, there's challenge and risk
On wilderness trails.

Across rushing streams, and up through the trees
The twisted path seems to take me with ease.
Then reaching the line where forest meets grass,
In golden sunshine the hours soon pass
On wilderness trails.

For this is my world; wild, open and free.
Like a flag unfurled, it thrills me to be
Where ramparts of rock, all sheathed in new snow,
Are my trade in stock wherever I go
On wilderness trails.

From steep cliff to ledge there echoes the cry
Of marmots on edge, because I'm so high.
The glare of the sun, the chill of the air,
Are part of the fun in tramping up there
On wilderness trails.

Here comes a fine buck strong in his prime
Oh wonderful luck to meet him this time.
Against the blue sky, on motionless wing
An eagle soars high; and makes my heart sing
On wilderness trails.

And now in the shade of evening twilight
A campfire is made and soon crackles bright.
With muscles at rest and mind all at ease,
I know life is best, whatever you please
On wilderness trails.

Contents

Books by W. Phillip Keller

Splendor from the Sea
As a Tree Grows
Bold Under God — Paul Bunyan of the West
A Shepherd Looks at Psalm 23
A Layman Looks at The Lord's Prayer
Rabboni — Which Is to Say, Master
A Shepherd Looks at the Good Shepherd and His Sheep
A Gardener Looks at the Fruits of the Spirit
Mighty Man of Valor — Gideon
Mountain Splendor
Taming Tension
Expendable
Still Waters
A Child Looks at Psalm 23
Ocean Glory
Walking with God
A Shepherd Looks at the Lamb of God
Elijah — Prophet of Power

About this Book

The whispering of forests under wind; the high faint cries of birds on wing; the murmur of sand and rocks under water; these are voices seldom heard in our radio broadcasts, schoolrooms, or television programmes. The bugling of elk in a wild glade, the thundering heads of 'bighorns' in battle, are sounds not heard beyond the rock ridges of their realm—never heard in the carpeted halls of our council chambers. The dancing hordes of wild flowers that fling themselves in cascades of colour across the alpine slopes seldom find reflection in the drab laws of the land. The majestic appeal of a mountain, that tugs at the heart of even the most callous human in its presence, makes few motions in Parliament.

That is why some of us who are fellow to the wilds feel compelled, in spite of ourselves, to shout aloud for them. Yesterday, today, and tomorrow we must continually be reminded of the priceless wilderness heritage entrusted to our care. That is the theme which runs through this work.

This book makes no pretence at being a profound reference work on Canadian wildlife. It is, rather, an honest attempt to share with the reader, some of the exhilaration, thrust, and thrill of life in the vigorous 'back country' of this continent. My genuine hope is that a little of the enthusiasm and inspiration which wild things and wilderness areas have poured into my life will spill over to those who read and perhaps encourage them to set out and taste further for themselves.

Somehow this generation must rediscover that the human heart can be lifted by free birds in flight; that the soul can draw strength from the noble solitude of mountain ramparts; that the mind can be refreshed with the untarnished beauty of an alpine meadow; that the body can gain vigour from the challenge of the trail and life under open skies.

It is for us all to remember that the earth does not belong to us. We belong to it. At best we are entrusted with a few brief years of life in which to relish the splendours about us. We are but an infinitesimal fragment of a staggering universe. It behoves us to cherish well those natural glories entrusted to our care. The humble knowledge that we have no claim upon them other than the honour of passing them on in at least as fine a form as we found them should lend honest dignity to our efforts on their behalf.

W. PHILLIP KELLER

1
Fairwinds

It had been another strenuous day: another day packed with conferences, business sessions, phone calls, and interviews. Just another day in the life of a business man. One's head pounded with the strain. The eternal rush was wearisome. What a life of superficiality it seemed: polished desks, cement sidewalks, the perpetual drum of typewriters within four mute walls. But here, suddenly thrust into my lap, were three golden hours of leisure. Three hours sandwiched between the last meeting and the time our boat was due to sail for the mainland.

What to do with those precious minutes that slipped away, irrepressible as the warm spring sun that dropped down towards the western horizon? Ah, that was easy to answer, for Chic and I revelled in a drive through the country. Both during our sweetheart days, and now as newly weds we secretly treasured the hours spent together in our favourite field and woodland haunts. The scenery of southern Vancouver Island would be rising to its finest on this balmy afternoon in mid-February, so away we went. Already the crocuses, snowdrops, yes, and even wild currants, were making a show of colour as we rolled leisurely past the spreading fields and natural parkland that bordered the open sea. Here and there the road wound through tall, cool stands of giant firs and cedars, interspersed with grey-barked balsam that flanked it like towering colonnades, casting broad shadows across the smooth, white gravel and filling the air with the pungent fragrance of woodland perfumes.

Almost without noticing it, we had turned down a narrow road that skirted a long arm of the sea. The limpid water reached up, far into the depths of a wooded valley. It sparkled blue wherever the sun touched it from behind the hills. We slowed down to admire the scene when suddenly the road emerged from the cool shadows of the timber to find us idling across the broad expanse of a rocky point that jutted out into the straights of Juan de Fuca. This jagged fragment of land, thrusting its dark head into the surf against the magnificent back-drop of the snow-capped Olympics, gripped our imagination. As we watched we felt drawn to follow the little winding trail to its very end, where our wheels touched the wave-washed sand.

Here every facet of Nature appeared completely in accord, so utterly serene. Every detail of the panorama perfectly integrated—the tender green of the grass by the road; a flock of brant that preened themselves on a gravel bar, split by the tide; overhead the white, drifting wings of gulls in flight.

'What a wonderful spot to live!' The exclamation expressed the deep emotion of our hearts that welled up through the silence that enveloped us in admiration. The glance that passed between us spoke volumes. Hastily we looked about. There was little evidence of life apart from some weatherbeaten shacks, presumably fishermen's shelters. The light grey boards told of wind and waves and sun.

But time did not stand still even though it seemed as if here Nature had remained static, unchanged from the beginning of time. Reluctantly we turned and started back, but the sea called loudly, begging us to pause and stay a while. Along the road we noticed, half buried in the undergrowth, half tumbled down, the remains of an old fence. Yes, and look, there an open field, once tilled but now grown up in native grass and ferns, fringed with wild roses, while beyond stretched a grove of trees, dark and green, looking almost black against the sky, and beyond that: Ah—there was no beyond, for all around lay the shimmering waters of the straits.

We pulled to the side of the road and stopped. An old, old homestead this! Was it abandoned? Had it been the dream of some aged couple who had struggled to hew for themselves a home from the wilderness? Or was it, like so many other things, merely forgotten, neglected, by-passed in the world's rush for bright and glittering things? Almost in fancy we could see it reaching out to us, asking for someone with an understanding heart, a kindly spirit, a brave courage to come and tend it, nourish it, cherish it, so that its fields would smile again, its woods ring with the joy of youth and life.

Slowly, irresistibly, we felt drawn to it. In its simple, rustic, yet alluring way, it beckoned to us. Here for the first time was a place, a piece of land that seemed to call us from the very depth of its dark, black soil. The only one that had struck a responsive chord during all those long years in which we had hoped, sought, yet never found.

'I wonder if it's for sale?' The words came involuntarily, the sentiment of two young hearts beating as one. It was Chic who spoke. How often while travelling on business we had followed advertisements, real-estate leads and myriad other clues in our restless search for the place of our dreams. But always it had been the same, 'Not for us!' spoken with a note of dismay, of futility, perhaps, but never defeat.

A little way up the road stood a neat, white cottage snuggled in the shelter of an old orchard. We stopped there to enquire of the cheery farmer's wife what story lay behind the place at the end of the road. She told us glibly, humorously, dramatically, until we felt we knew it like an old friend. Best of all, 'It is for sale,' she said, 'and very reasonable, too.'

'Enough, enough,' we thought. Carefully we had garnered and

17

gathered, saved and scrimped for a sum that some day was to lay the foundation of our future life. What better footing, we pondered, could be found in which to root ourselves than the warmth, feeling, and live response of this humble old place with its gnarled oaks, wind-bent pines, grassy slopes, and rock-bound bays.

We turned back to it briefly. Just one more convincing look. So we crossed the pastures, followed the shore, tramped the woods. The sun was setting. Time was short. Together now we stood on a rugged bluff above the sea. A breath of evening air ruffled the water. I put my arm about Chic. This was our moment of decision. Quietly she looked up into my face. 'I love it here,' she said with a smile.

'Then it's ours,' I replied, hugging her to me.

Just a little more than one month later, a month packed with the feverish activity of rounding off my work at the office and terminating the business in hand, we were down at the old homestead, getting better acquainted so we could lay our plans for the coming year.

What joyous, carefree, boisterous days those were. Out in the wind, the salt spray and the sun; free as the wisps of tattered clouds that scudded across the sky. Away from the grind of office routine; relieved from the perpetual pressure of responsibility; released in the atmosphere of total abandon, youthful spirits rebounded with vigour and buoyancy.

For several days we roamed eagerly over the acres of unkempt fields and woods, every one waiting to be explored, waiting to show us some secret, long hidden, known only to itself. Here was an old earth dam where once there had been a pond. Over in the heart of the woods was a crab-apple swamp; happy hunting ground for coons, the favourite haunt of mallards. Down at the bottom of the old pasture a freshwater pond, once stocked with trout, was now merely the home for a family of otter. An empty cabin that would do to live in for the summer stood by a little bay on the shore, complete with a rusty stove, an old oak rocking-chair, and one apple box. From a well, dug years before, we drew clear, cold water, crystal pure. Along the beach great piles of driftwood, logs, boards, bark, bottles, yes—and even planks lay where the waves had thrown them.

With every new discovery our spirits soared. With each new day our faith mounted. It would be a hardy, yes, a crude life mayhap, by some standards, but for us a full one, a satisfying measure, pressed down with good things, overflowing with simple happiness.

Our wee cabin soon became our mansion. Perched on the water's edge its windows were awash with the rising sun that splashed its colours on the bay at dawn. The same bay that at dusk softened to a flood of mellow moonlight. A pair of swallows that nested beneath the eaves, often swooped in through open windows to light on the rafters overhead and arch their chirpy heads in curious wonderment.

The season was getting on, perhaps too far along to put in a garden, we thought, but why not try? Feverishly we turned the wild, tough, sod. It came up black, rich, smooth like velvet to the touch. The feel of good damp earth, lying upturned to the sunshine, was a thrill in itself. That alone reassured us, and in simple trust we staked the rows, planted the seed. Little did we imagine the plenteous harvest we would gather from the bosom of that patch. The heaping bowls of salad, deep with lettuce, tomatoes, radishes, and cucumbers; those bulging sacks of potatoes, turnips, and carrots piled in the old wood-shed safe from frost; the gleaming rows of pickles, relish, and preserves lining the pantry shelves, reserved against the cold, unyielding days of winter; all amply confirmed our faith in the land. Even the big-bellied crocks of salted beans, sauerkraut, and dills reassured us of a bountiful table when winter gales whipped in from the north. The land had responded to our caress, given generously from her storehouse.

Swiftly, softly, the summer months sped by. It was a joy to be in the brilliant sunshine reflected brightly from the sparkling, glittering breadth of ocean. Our skins exposed to the tang of salt air and biting wind, tingled, turning to a beautiful brown under the spell of tempting warmth. Our work became an adventure every day, each hour all too short for all we planned to do. Life was keen, zestful. It whetted our appetites, sharpened our minds. Life was hard, vigorous. We had to use our wits, our heads, our hands. Night came swiftly, heralded by glorious sunsets that brandished their flaming colours in flaunted banners across the western sky. Weary, yet happy; stiff sometimes, we found our beds welcome, for sleep came easily, gently, refreshing as the silver dew that lay upon the grass at dawn.

Almost like a thief, fall crept over the country, but we were ready for her. The fences had been repaired, new drainage ditches dug,

 19

the harvest stored. Even now, a new road, graded and gravelled, led to the cottage where we planned our winter home.

There we worked feverishly with hammer, saw, and brush; repairing, adding, tearing down, dismantling—converting from a shack to a home, by sheer dint of work and the material found at hand, gathered from beach, woods, and shed. Here a board, there a window, the remains of an old table, part of a shipwreck, all were incorporated within the framework of the home. Late into the night, often into the morning hours the sound of tools on timber echoed across the darkness from the shore. Slowly, imperceptibly the rooms took shape, every nook and corner used to best advantage for shelves, cupboards, and racks.

Bravely, stoutly, Chic wielded the brush, stroke after stroke, dip upon dip, while her baby lay fast asleep in a bunk built of driftwood in one corner of the cabin. But look, inexorably the framework yields to our efforts. It takes on new form, new beauty. Here a home is moulded, fashioned in love, in tenderness; every swinging stroke bringing it closer to the line; every blow bending it to our will. Within its walls are crude, rough, unfinished boards; beneath its coat of paint odds and ends that had been a motley sight. None the less, she grows apace until—until at last we stand back to view the humble masterpiece. Our look is one of endearment. 'Let's call it Balsam Bungalow,' and so we named our home. Nestled among the balsams and oaks the little cottage appeared friendly, warm, appealing; cosy with an atmosphere of comfort and quiet contentment. For a long moment we stood silent, watching in the twilight, then with mutual feeling we turned to kiss each other, a fitting, fervent climax to our common effort.

The following day we moved. Our plain furnishings in the summer cabin were few and light. For Chic, as for every woman everywhere, it was a thrill to fill the empty cupboards, the bare shelves; to hang the curtains, arrange the pictures, flowers, nick-nacks, and other feminine touches that make home a home with loved ones to share it. Then, too, there were boxes of books to unpack, along with the rifles, rods, ammunition, and binoculars; each had an allotted space. Just moving; moving into a home all our own, not only because we owned it, but because we had made it a part of ourselves was a thrill that knew no bounds. How far removed, how estranged from the milling masses that haunt apartment blocks and crowd the rooms of roaring cities. This was bliss.

That very night winter broke loose. Venting its pent-up fury on the rocky coast it hurled gigantic waves against the jagged rocks. The surging surf boomed and thundered in the darkness. Foam hissed and ran up across the sand; white-caps plumed into spray with the shrieking force of the gale that whipped at them angrily. The flying spume howled through the trees, whined in the chimney. The roof moaned a trifle when the wind sucked at the eaves. Now and then the cottage shook, struck with a sudden, stormy surge of wind that made her tremble. We crawled down under the covers, drew them close and tight about our heads. We laughed gaily and threw back a taunt into the teeth of the storm. The driving sleet spattered and rattled against the window spasmodically. Fiercer and fiercer the gale mounted until it shrieked in a rising crescendo of terror. Suddenly it died, a lull, but in the lull we slept. Our home had stood the storm.

Winter came cool. The long evenings were filled with books, with music, with friends, with writing. Here was time for pleasant relaxation, for mental rejuvenation. Here was opportunity to polish dulled brains, to furbish old acquaintances, to renew friendly feelings with literature, art, and music.

Even the short, dull days spent with axe, saw, and wedges in the woods were not without interest; the aroma of freshly cut pine; the pale-blue smoke from a fire of alder limbs; the crisp feel of filed teeth cutting through logs of fir and balsam gave a sense of well-being. The blood raced in the cold air. One anticipated eagerly those hearty meals of venison stew or fresh clam chowder, rich with vegetables and spices.

And so a year had nearly rolled around. A year fully satisfying, a year of deep delight. A time of integration; of discovering one's true self. A time of developing self-confidence; self-reliance; of identifying oneself with a place, the soil, the land. It had repaid our love, our interest a hundredfold. It had taught us the fundamental, basic things of life that have faded from modern thought. We placed new emphasis on new values, for there are values in life other than dollars and cents. In fact, they had become so real, so tangible to our senses that we could not part with them for they were part of us.

21

What could one pay for the clear, lucid notes of a song sparrow rippling across a meadow on a spring morning? Or what could be exchanged for the joyous chorus of a thousand voices singing from the shore where a host of sandpipers chant at dusk? What is the price to pay for the sight of white wings wheeling gracefully against the blue sky, blue sea; or the cost of a single glimpse at early dawn of sun-tinted peaks draped in snow. These were the secrets of our life—exhilarating, bounding, carefree life.

Then it was spring again. The willows were full-blown, the grass was greening, mouthed eagerly by our band of sheep. The wild currants, too, started to bloom and the cherries to bud. The sky was cloudless, the sea white-capped, ruffled with the wind. Always wind, yes, but we loved the wind. It blew away the clouds. It left the air fresh, the earth sun-drenched. That, you see, is why we called this place, this first farm of ours, Fair-Winds.

2
Salmon Stream

TO STOOP LOW and bury my face in the fast running water of a crystal stream, there to drink deeply of the clear cool liquid is one of my favourite delights in outdoor life on this continent. I indulge in this pleasure at every opportunity, nor has its sensation of deep satisfaction ever waned.

This can be explained by the very simple fact that half my life has been spent in parts of Africa which were hot and arid. Places where water, any kind of water, was a precious horded substance. More often

than not the muddy liquid, whether drawn from a river, water-hole, or well, had the appearance of murky tea with a taste obnoxious to the white man's palate.

Most important, though, was the fact that one dared not put it to his lips without first boiling away what true water flavour it might have had originally, leaving it a flat repulsive drink. But this had to be, since Africans, their cattle and sheep, besides untold game animals, had perforce to all drink, bathe, and disport themselves in the same water. As needful and inviting as any stream might appear to the hot and thirst-tortured traveller in Africa it could also be his deadly enemy as a carrier of disease.

Little wonder then that I love to plunge my head into our glorious gushing streams. To open my eyes and peer through the sparkling flow at the rock-strewn bed; to listen to its song; to drink and drink and drink.

Apart from this, our northern streams, especially those that I am familiar with in this rugged north-west country, have a verve and vitality foreign to the majority of sluggish waterways common to the African bush country. This liveliness has a strong fascination that compels one to return again and again, if for no other reason than the sheer sensual sights and sounds it produces.

In winter with heavy ocean swells thundering on the beaches; with grey blankets of rain saturating the watersheds; with the valleys turbulent under a load of rushing run-off, hurrying back to the sea the streams become an angry aggressive force in the land.

The water is moody and dark and dangerous. It cuts and jabs at banks and bends, tearing away the soil, uprooting trees, and loosening rocks. A tangled burden of woodland wreckage is carried along relentlessly. The persistent pressure of the current piles up dams of debris that suddenly burst, releasing tons of water that rampage down the valleys gouging out still more trees, logs, and roots that are disgorged at the river mouths into the waiting basin of the sea. There the flotsam is picked up on grey waves and tossed back to the land to form necklaces of driftwood that encircle the beaches at highwater mark.

With spring sunshine the pace quickens, especially if the stream originates with a mountain snowfield or glacier bed. But soon the freshet is over, with the lesser flow the water clears. Silt finds time to settle in the current; and fish swirl at the surface, taking early hatches of insects that can be readily seen through the clear water.

Word spreads that the fish are taking a lure and up and down the banks ardent anglers whip their favourite pools and races.

Not to be outdone by his human counterpart, the rattle-throated cry of the kingfisher declares his private rights to a portion of the stream that he has staked for himself. His undulating flight of patrol up and down the watery avenue beneath the overhanging trees is a continual reminder to intruders that here he will not share his fishing rights with any other feathered intruder. Eagles, hawks, crows, or ravens will all be attacked irrespective of their reason for visiting the stream.

As spring slips into summer, coons and bears forage along the banks. Earlier the bears had fed on the skunk cabbages that pushed their golden spikes through the murky ooze at the water's edge. Now they hunt for crabs, snails, or any other morsel that the flowing stream might have brought down from its upper reaches.

Small fry will be feeding in the waters, too, some of them making their precarious journey down towards the powerful pull of the great salt sea where they will grow to the full strength of their species.

Under summer sun and heat the forest smells strongly of resin, pitch, and conifer needles. The warmth settles down into the under storey of the woods where salmon berries and blackberries set fruit that will swell and ripen. Wild bees and bumble-bees drone across the water in search of nectar; wasps and hornets flit down to drink on the mud banks and sand bars.

Under blue skies the stream shrinks. The gay running laughter of of spring drifts into the murmuring music of summer water slipping across smooth stones from one deep pool to the next.

Sometimes, in these deep pools near the mouth of the river, silver salmon will await the fall freshets. Their bodies are thick and turgid with milt and roe. This was the stream of their birth. Depending upon their species, they will have been away in the ocean depths for several years and now return to their home waters, drawn irresistibly by the instinct to perpetuate their kind.

Those salmon not up in the pools will hover about the mouth of the stream, waiting for the rising pressure of fresh water against their sides; waiting for the chemical stimuli, borne to them on the current of their parent stream, to start that last upwards trek to the spawning grounds, from which there is no return.

This long trip from ocean deep to gravel bed has been fraught with danger for the silver beauties. First the trawlers out where the run commenced in the broad Pacific: Then the seiners and gillnetters as their hordes crowded into the narrowing straits and channels of the coast: Now, at the river mouth, sportsmen take a heavy toll of the massed, impatient fish.

Then, one autumn afternoon, rain sweetens the sun-dried land. Slowly, water percolates through the forest floor to feed the stream. The fresh cool flow recharges the sluggish summer stream with oxygen and new vigour. Its level rises and fish start to fight their way into the swelling current.

Not only is the water moving now; a fierce up-hill movement is under way, too; the current of life that must find its origin if it is to survive. The stream resounds to the splash and swirl of driving desperate bodies intent on reaching the gravel beds where the eggs will be shed and fertilized.

It is an ancient drama this, the epic ebb and flow of life up and down the stream. The exhausted fish, their life purpose fulfilled, hang limp in the shallows or drift back to the banks where their bruised bodies pollute the air.

Drawn by the sight and smell, bears, gulls, ravens, eagles, and crows congregate along the water's edge, gorging on the feast that will fatten them for the lean dark winter ahead. For soon the rising winds, drenching rains, and high winter water will remove the last trace of the stream's silver horde.

3
Bird Sanctuary

SOME of the most arresting experiences which contributed to my interest in wildlife preservation have been recounted in preceeding chapters. Although they occurred at different times, under a wide range of conditions and with various types of wildlife, they were like parallel lines of force which drove me irresistibly towards a single destination in life.

That was an attempt to establish a true bird sanctuary of my own.

The world famous efforts of Jack Miner on his farm in southern Ontario had always gripped my imagination. The manner in which the Canada geese especially responded to his love and protection is a story so well known that it requires no repetition here.

The unusual coincidence in my desire to establish a similar refuge at Fair-Winds, was our geographical locations. Just as Jack Miner's farm was on the southernmost extension of Canadian soil in the east, so we were situated on the southernmost tip of Canadian land in the west —both sites were below the 49th parallel and both were on strategic migratory flyways.

I would not be so brash as to state that I had all these features in mind while I searched for a farm. Rather it was a set of happy circumstances that favoured us in our choice of land. Its location from a wildlife, more especially bird standpoint, proved to be better by far than one would normally hope to find.

By looking back now across the span of time to those five fruitful years spent working with the wild creatures, I cannot help but feel that it was an act of benevolent Providence that led us there in the first place.

Although Fair-Winds constituted little else than a derelict, run-down bit of countryside when we bought it, there was a potential power to recuperate hidden beneath its abused appearance. I sensed this with an uncanny feeling from the first moment that I set foot upon its impoverished fields. What I did not realize was how thrilling would be its come-back under our care.

For birds in particular the 200-odd acres offered an assortment of terrain that would attract an exceedingly wide variety of feathered friends. Surrounded as it was on two sides by the sea—some of the shoreline being mudflats and shallows—this was a great attraction for shore birds. Off shore there were islands and lonely rock outcrops frequented by numerous sea-birds and used as nesting-sites.

On the farm was our little lake that drew its quota of fresh-water species. The great open fields were home to upland birds, while the thick forested acres, reedy marshland, and dry parkland each attracted its own denizens. It was not altogether too surprising then to discover that eventually some eighty-five different species had been identified on the farm.

Fair-Winds was unique, too, in its soil. That is, in so far as coastal land was concerned. Its fields had not all been cleared with axes, fires, and teams from the dense virgin timber of the coastal rain forest.

Rather it was a part of a very small area on the southern tip of Vancouver Island where the unusual Garry Oak, Madrone (Arbutus) association of trees prevailed. Here a semi-parkland type of forest had allowed a rich grass sward to survive. Under this sod rich black prairie soil had developed as distinct from the brownish clay forested earth common to other regions of the coast.

It was good, rich, deep, dark earth. With careful husbandry it again became covered with a verdant mantle of thick, lush grass. With the healing of the land the birds and wild creatures began to return. In a manner known to them, but long lost to civilized man, they could detect the increasing fertility in the feed from those acres. With this knowledge they began to flock back.

In fact my neighbour once remarked to me that the pheasants all seemed to stay on my side of the road. When I told him why, he was kind enough not to laugh in my face, though I knew in his heart he thought me a fool. This was because he had been born and raised on his farm and for over forty years had done exactly as his father had done —mined it out—only a little faster with the help of power equipment.

But it was not only pheasants that came back to make up for those distressing days when I had watched them slaughtered in the skies over Lulu Island. The grouse came back, too.

These were the willow grouse or as the same bird is known in the east, 'the drummer' or ruffled grouse. One old cock in particular beat a path into our very hearts with his rumbling tattoo on a favourite log just back of the kitchen door. He would start this ritual before winter ever gathered up her white skirts and retreated north. Even at two in the morning the throbbing sound would echo from the log, nor would he desist until late in the spring.

One of the truly thrilling birds which were a rarity in this part of the planet were some English skylarks which had adapted themselves after having been imported from Britain. Their lavish song as they heralded summer's arrival was a theme not soon forgotten.

Perhaps one of the most rewarding sights I ever saw was one evening when I discovered a very large solitary bird strutting across the biggest field on the farm. A careful stalk disclosed that he was a sandhill crane. He stayed several days, and in subsequent years he brought others until the last time I saw them a flight of seventeen circled over-

head before gliding down to alight where he had stood alone that second year after our arrival.

During the Second World War the magnificent trumpeter swans of this continent were perilously close to extinction. My interest in them was whetted to a very high degree when an intimate friend of mine was appointed manager of the Red Rock Lakes Trumpeter Swan Refuge in Montana. We corresponded at length about the birds, and eventually I was able to spend several glorious days with him on the refuge on my way to Africa.

To my amazement I discovered a pair of these birds on a swamp that adjoined our land. It was the first occasion in many years that these regal birds had been seen in that part of the country.

With careful protection and much publicity for their preservation the trumpeter has staged a fairly steady comeback, until today it is estimated that there are some 1,500 of the birds in British Columbia alone.

It was through these birds that contact was made with the Canadian federal wildlife authorities. Gradually, there began to take shape in my mind the concept of a proper wildlife sanctuary under federal jurisdiction. This was necessary if the sea and shore birds were to be protected, since all tidal waters are open to the public for boating, fishing, shooting, or recreation.

Not only were we situated on the main Pacific flyway of the migratory birds, but our sheltered coves, bays, and mudflats provided an ideal wintering ground for resident species.

Naturally such an ideal place for the ducks and geese was well known to local hunters who, in the past, had made it a veritable hell for the birds. So much so that they had learned to avoid it, except for the hours of darkness when scattered flights would drop in to feed.

Efforts for the first few years to establish a proper sanctuary were thwarted by opposition from the local hunters. Had the birds been edible and fit for food the picture would have been much different, for I would have seen a reason for the slaughter. As it was, by far the greater percentage of those shot were sea-ducks or fish-eaters which, no matter how carefully prepared, were decidedly disagreeable to the taste.

This I knew from experience since we had tried them ourselves, using all the tricks in the trade to render their flesh palatable. Soaking in salt water; stuffing with potatoes, apples, carrots, or raisins; even skinning them, scarcely helped at all.

4
Pheasant Shooting

PHEASANT shooting, like the unhappy duck-hunting experiences of Ontario, perhaps had as much to do with redirecting my energies from the pursuit of wildlife to its preservation as any other force of which I have knowledge.

This was not because I felt that these beautiful birds were in danger of extermination. After all, they are not a native to this continent, but an import of Oriental origin. The pheasant has found an environment well suited to its needs in many regions of the continent. Where this occurs it flourishes to the point of dominating the local field of upland game birds.

This I discovered quite by chance during the summer that I left California to look for work in the north-west. En route I had stopped in eastern Oregon to see if I could obtain some seasonal work in the great pea and wheat country around a tiny tumbled-down town with the pretentious name of Athena.

Until this time my only acquaintance with the regal ring-neck had been either in books or perchance an occasional glimpse of one planing low across some distant cornfield as I drove across the corn-belt of the mid-west.

But in Athena this all changed. If it could boast of little else in those far-off days, at least it could lay claim to being a perfect pheasant paradise. The vast patchwork quilt of interlocking fields rich with peas and ripening grain was aglow with the colourful birds. They were everywhere—not singly or in pairs, but whole flocks and flights of them.

It was my custom to sleep under the stars by the roadside. With the brief night of summer in this northerly latitude, hours of sleep were something precious and rare that one snatched between the time these proud birds relaxed their chatter in the late twilight until the first hint of dawn set them off in fresh cascades of calling.

Perhaps it is different now. Pheasant shooting enjoys a tremendous following today, and those mellow fields where the pheasants held un-disputed sway twenty years ago, have, without doubt, reverberated to the thunder of a thousand shotguns. These canny birds learn quickly, and it would not surprise me if they are now less prone to declare their whereabouts to all the wide world. When in my roadside bed-roll I was the only human for mayhap a dozen miles—they had virtually no fear of man.

It is odd that my next intimate encounter, several years later, with these feathered creatures should have been almost the exact opposite of the first. Irked and feeling shackled by the duties that bound me to a city desk for a short time, I welcomed any chance to flee the confines of four brick walls. This came unexpectedly one day with an invitation from my superintendent to go pheasant hunting on Lulu Island, a short drive out from Vancouver.

My companion even loaned me a gun, explained that he had secured the shooting rights on a friend's, farm and assured me that opening day would be a merry one for us.

In my mind I pictured ourselves strolling nonchalantly across broad meadows with dogs working hard in advance to flush the birds. The prospects of such a glorious outing in the autumn sunshine was a treat to contemplate.

Opening day found us on the allotted farm; having quite literally fought our way out there in a bumper-to-bumper duel with two or three thousand other hunters. Everyone was in full fighting trim; red caps, red hats, red vests, red shirts, red jackets—yes, even red shotgun shells, boxes and boxes of them. There were a good many red faces, too, from sundry causes, flashes of temper, flushes of anticipation, and flasks in hip pockets.

To my astonishment we had to share the farm, only about thirty acres of flat colourless land, criss-crossed with deep drainage ditches and bordered by dykes, with about a dozen other men, none of whom seemed to know each other. To top things off, roads and fences surrounding the place were dotted with men and dogs of assorted sizes and stamp.

As I recall it the zero hour came at precisely eleven o'clock. Men paced uneasily up and down their chosen beats, fingering firearms, and watching watches. Then it happened. There was a blast of shot from behind the farmhouse and I saw a lone cock fly up out of the farmer's cabbage patch and sail towards the dyke. A dozen shells burst around him before he fluttered to a heap in a ditch.

I ducked into a ditch myself as shot pattered about me. Ahead of me another cock pheasant, his body pressed to the ground, squirmed along through the grass trying to conceal himself.

Almost before I spotted him I felt a blast of shot go past my head and cut into the grass. It was a close shave and I fell flat as a second burst whipped past me and caught the bird just as he was clearing the bank.

I got up and turned to see where the firing had come from. A youth, obviously a city boy on his first hunt, was standing in the ditch twenty yards behind me. He looked angry and ready to fight, not with me, but because two other men had already rushed to pick up the fallen bird. I really don't know who shot it. I do know the lad was out his pheasant but in on a goodly share of homely advice from me on how to handle a gun in future.

The office dream had become a nightmare. Disgusted I drew the shells from the breech and went back to wait in the car.

Happily enough this was the last occasion I ever ran into this crowded hunting. But it did set me to thinking. In subsequent years I enjoyed fine pheasant shooting in the Okanagan Valley, always enlivened by the superb scenery and setting of that ornate orchard country.

Yet it seemed each fall there were getting to be fewer birds and more hunters. Finally a turning point was reached one evening when I was alone with my dog on a 5,000-acre ranch in the dry-belt country that boasted some of the best pheasant shooting in British Columbia.

By request a group of business men had arranged to hunt the ranch that day. Before they started each had been asked to abide strictly by the game laws and to show the highest calibre of sportsmanship in their outing.

Mid-afternoon found the entire group reassembled, each with his limit bag, much elated and ready to return to the city. When they left I started out to cover the spots I knew the birds favoured.

Without firing a shot my old dog recovered over a dozen cocks that had been killed without being picked up. Besides these I bagged a number of crippled birds that would have been left to suffer until death or a coyote ended their misery.

This little episode crystallized my thinking about the plight of our birds. There would always be hunters—that I knew—at least as long as there was something left to hunt. But I, for my part, determined that if ever a day came when I owned a bit of land of my own, it would be set aside as a sanctuary for the birds. It was the least I could do as a token of my affection for my feathered friends.

So, when we acquired Fair-Winds we lost no time in carrying out this plan.

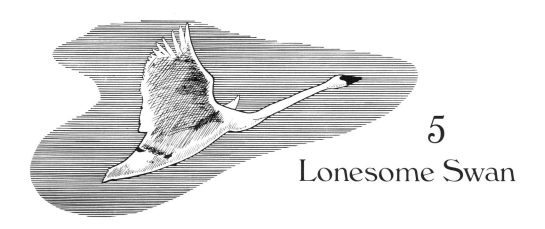

5
Lonesome Swan

THE long low howl of a steady wind moaned down the broad valley floor. It brooded over the barren sands of the dry lake bed—grasping, lifting, then moving them relentlessly into tiny drifts and dunes. With passing seasons and the eternal pressure of the moving air great ridges of sand hills had been shaped to split the surface of the landscape. There poplars, spruce, and mountain juniper struggled grimly to throw a live mantle over the shifting soil.

These ridges formed a natural and, for all wildlife, an attractive route from one mountain basin to another. In the soft sand were to be

found such a display of animal tracks as to quicken the pulse and widen the eye. Elk and bear, deer and coyote, cougar and otter, squirrel and chipmunk, birds and insects—all had left mute signs of their passing steps.

So it was there that I had chosen to secrete my camp. Hidden by the side of this wilderness highway I would watch the mixed stream of passersby—a marvellous place for wildlife photography.

The first morning that I took up my watch my eye caught a mere speck of white drifting on the surface of a marshy lake in the distance. Scrutinizing it with my binoculars from the crest of the ridge I could see that it was a swan, a lone swan!

The sight excited me. Swans, especially wild swans, had always stirred my imagination. I thrilled to the lift and beat of their wide wings carrying them across the high mountain valleys of the west. They were such a magnificent part of those remote wilderness areas where heavy human feet seldom trod.

There lingered in my mind's eye the haunting sight of the great white Trumpeter swans I had watched drifting placidly on the wild marshlands of northern Montana, their glistening plumage iridescent against a superb backdrop of golden tulles and sapphire water. Out there in a clear October sky I had seen them soaring majestically in pairs with rhythmic wing beat and trumpet call. They, like this solitary bird I watched, were but a fragment of the splendid flocks that once adorned the continent. No wonder a twinge of sadness crept into my heart as I hoped against hope that perhaps this one's mate would appear, but none did.

During the days that I stalked the ridges of sand in search of elk and deer or skirted the lakeshore for moose and beaver pictures, the swan had often seen me. At first, like all of his kind, he was wary and timid and held to the centre of the lake.

With frequent encounters he seemed to sense that I was too busy with other game to wish him any harm. So it was, that after several days, at my approach he would momentarily raise his head erect, give me a sharp piercing glance, as if to say, 'Oh yes, the same fellow again!' then bury his head amid the feathers on his back and drift off to sleep.

One cold windy afternoon I had been following moose tracks along the edge of a willow bottom near my camp. Suddenly on peering around a clump of brush I spotted the swan resting on a mud-bank at the water's edge. For three seconds I stood overwhelmed. What a chance for a fine photograph, but it would entail skilful stalking!

For an hour and a half I crept, crawled, and slid on my belly like a weasel in the grass. Every time the alert bird lifted his head I lay still as death, the beat of my heart hammering in my throat lest he fly and leave me disappointed. At last the glistening white body filled the viewfinder of the camera against a bold background of broken peaks and blue water. Gently I whistled so that he would lift his head from its resting place between his wings. For a fleeting moment he was poised and proud. In that instant of grandeur his beauty was captured. He detected the snap of the shutter, but did not fly. Instead he gave me a long searching stare as though he thought: 'It's you again.' Then drifted placidly away from the mud-bar into deeper water.

My clothes were stained and askew from the long earthy stalk. My face and hands were hot with perspiration from the tension and thrill. But in my heart there glowed a feeling of warmth and friendly contact with this denizen of the wilds.

While I sat on the bank reflecting on the unique experience the great bird floated gracefully in front of me, making no effort whatever to leave. In fact, as I collected my feelings I sensed that somehow he was lonely and actually found solace in the strange companionship of this human being who sat there in silent admiration. It was a mysteriously beautiful sensation this. Somehow to have bridged the gap and found oneself *en rapport* with this bird. So I sat and talked to him while the wind ruffled the feathers in his plumage. Often before in photographing and working with wildlife I had talked to animals—lions in particular in Africa, deer in the Olympics, and mountain sheep in the Rockies, but never before to a bird, a wild untamed bird.

Thus we enjoyed the pleasure of each other's company until the distant bugling of a bull elk distracted my attention. It was with a feeling bordering on real regret that I decided to take my leave and go in the direction of the elk's mating challenge. As I walked away it was with a deep conviction that the bird and I would meet again.

The steady wind that blew incessantly down the giant valley shifting the sand, tried hard to move my tent in the night. Only stout logs laid over the ground ropes kept it from following the flying grains of sand. In the wind, too, were long dagger darts of early winter cold that cut through the tent, sleeping-bag, and woollen clothes to probe and punish bones and blood. Especially blood that was thin and poor from the hot African plains and years of malaria. Camp had to be broken. There was no choice, even though game was all about.

Up before dawn, as has always been my habit when in the field, I wandered down to a small slough near the camp to watch the sunrise —my last sunrise at this camp. It came flaming, with banners, behind the black ridges. I caught its glow on the surface of the tiny pond, and there snuggled at its edge among the reeds was my friend the swan. He was barely a stone's throw from where I had slept. Gently I moved towards him, hoping he would swim out where I could photograph his form silhouetted against the rising sun. But he did not move. Loath to disturb him I passed by, resolving to come back to visit him when the light was bright.

This I did. Still he lingered in the reeds on the bank. I approached him softly, murmuring a greeting. Closer and closer, still he hovered in front of me. Scarcely could I believe that he was now within arm's reach. Just then he turned his head towards me. There was a slow halting motion to it. Then it faltered, collapsed sideways, and he died before my very feet.

I stood stunned.

Deeply moved I turned away in grief. Painfully I retraced my steps to the nearby tent to break camp.

In some mysterious, unknown manner beyond the senses of a mere man, was this magnificent creature of the wilds aware that I was leaving him to be alone again?

This is a question I dare not answer.

6
Getting My Goat

THE Rocky Mountain Goat, really not a goat at all but a member of the antelope species, was, apart from deer, one of the first North American big-game animals I encountered in my mountain trips.

On that occasion, instead of being a dextrous daredevil who performed incredible feats of rock work on rugged ridges, he left me with quite the opposite impression. I was clambering about some rugged crags on Mount Rainier when in a tiny green glen far below me I spotted a group of thirty-six goats grazing on the grass sward. They

were so minute at that distance they might well have been daisies, mobile flowers moving across the carpet of alpine greenery.

Hastily I scrambled down the cliffs and crept on hands and stomach until I was less than 100 yards from the flock. It was not too long before they bedded down in a cluster about a small grove of alpine firs. I lay still in the grass watching this tranquil scene until the lengthening shadows filled the valleys with darkness and warned me to turn towards camp.

First impressions in life are quite often the most enduring. That charming alpine setting with the contented creatures resting on its greenery has never faded from my mind, even though in subsequent years I have seen goats in much more harsh surroundings.

When first I set about serious wildlife photography in North America, goats were one species which I felt would be interesting to work with because of the rough terrain they lived in. My aim in taking pictures of game is always to portray the animal itself in a setting that will convey a little of the 'feeling' or 'atmosphere' of its habitat and everyday existence. This is not always easy to do. In fact it would be much more simple to use very powerful lenses and concentrate on animal portraits. This has become quite a common practice with many wildlife photographers. One can readily discern this type of picture by the blurred foreground and background both of which may be more or less out of focus, depending upon the magnification of the lens and the distance at which the picture was taken. It is true this may make for a 'spectacular' shot that impresses audiences, but to my mind it is very much less attractive or informative than one which depicts the creature in his natural surroundings.

This may have been somewhat of a digression from goats, but I felt it is appropriate here since they are a species in which the challenge to achieve my type of photograph can be most exciting.

With this prospect in mind I decided to try and obtain pictures of goats in a region where the species was not native but had been introduced. The wardens of the area gave me little encouragement, stating that their naturalists had been attempting to secure pictures of the animals for two years with very little success.

My two initial efforts were likewise not only fruitless but almost fatal. After all one cannot hope for goats on flower fields all the time, and I knew if I was to succeed the craggy peaks would have to be my hunting range.

The very first attempt I made to stalk a nanny and her kid brought me down a steep incline to where she had taken up her look-out under a scrubby spruce that overhung a canyon. By patient manœuvring I managed to get within fourteen feet of her, with only the protecting tree between us. The wily old girl spotted me and plunged down the canyon, to what I was sure could be only certain death. A few moments later, amid the rumble of rubble and rolling rocks, she scrambled up out of the depths on the other side, her kid close behind. That was the last I ever saw of the pair. All that I had to show for the adventure was a mediocre shot of the pair climbing across the distant rock face. But my respect for a goat's mountaineering skill increased 50 per cent.

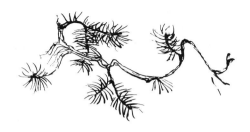

The next occasion I tackled a peak with the picturesque title of Storm King Mountain. Its narrow ledges and wind-dwarfed shrubbery showed few signs of the goats I had been told made it their refuge.

What started out as an innocent search for goat pictures very soon degenerated into a scramble to survive from the nightmarish predicament in which I found myself. The entire upper portion of this eminence was composed of 'rotten' rock. As anyone knows who has climbed on such material, it offers more danger per square foot than a minefield.

In a foolhardy attempt to force myself up a chimney near the summit I dislodged chunks of rotten rock that began to break away all around me in an alarming fashion. Worst of all their bouncing, banging action precipitated a minor avalanche of rolling sliding material that threatened to tear away a good chunk of the mountain below my very boots. The prospect of being hurled and tossed down that chute with tons of rubble rolling me into a pulp on the way was not altogether a happy thought.

Eventually, by digging away with toe and fingers at the crumbling face, I was able to excavate tiny hand and footholds that left me clinging to them breathlessly. Inch by inch I worked my way spider-like down that desperate draw. With feet firmly on a goat trail again I was content to leave those hardy denizens to their dizzy heights. By now my respect for goats was a full 100 per cent.

If I could not succeed here I was determined to try again elsewhere. My third attempt was to bear out the truth of that old saying: 'Third time always lucky.'

43

The next remote, wind-swept ridge I tackled was of solid granite. The hard rock gave me great confidence. So did the frequent signs I came across of goat hair clinging to bushes; dust baths and numerous tracks. I had cached an extra supply of food at the top of the ridge. The skies were clear, portending several days of fine weather, and deep in my bones I felt this trip would click!

The high spirits in which I set out began to fade as the day wore on. Ahead of me there loomed a giant draw in the ridge, beyond this I simply could not go since my way was blocked by a massive wall of perpendicular rock up which I could see no possible route. Had it not been for the glorious sunshine that flooded the entire panorama about me this obstacle would have been most depressing.

I felt confident that the rock wall was not insuperable to goats. So when I reached the edge of the gaping divide I resigned myself to the thought that I was to be thwarted again. In wildlife photography one has to be mentally prepared to accept repeated rebuffs.

It was late afternoon, and I had negotiated roughly nine miles of broken country. A rest would be refreshing. I scrambled to a projecting rock that overhung a small swale lying in the shadows below. There I could get a better view of the wild sweep of country about me while I rested.

Peering down I was astounded to see a goat and her kid grazing in the gloomy depths some 1,500 feet below me. It was too late to try and get down to her. In any case there would never be enough light in that hole even at noon.

A flash of inspiration struck me. I let out a shrill piercing whistle like the warning cry of a marmot. The goat and the kid bounded for the rocks and scrambled to the top of a huge boulder standing in less deep shadows. It was an interesting pose even if poorly lit. I waited anxiously about the interval of time a marmot does if not sure of danger, then whistled again. The goats bounded upward and I was thrilled to see them joined by three others.

They worked their way to some narrow ledges where I assumed they would stay, because it seemed impossible for them to come up any farther on such steep faces. Since they were now within distant camera range I manœuvred in and out of the ledges attempting to get a little closer but found myself always cut off by sheer cliffs.

I decided to backtrack and try a different approach from another side. Hardly had I gone back more than a dozen paces when up out of the very mouth of the chasm emerged the old nanny. I was positively dumbfounded. How did she ever negotiate those perpendicular walls?

I froze in my tracks. A moment later her kid jumped up beside her. The only sensible explanation I can give for what transpired during the next few minutes is that emerging from the dark depths their eyes were unaccustomed to the bright glare of sunshine up on top where I stood.

The old nanny appeared not to see me at first. I focused on her and then she started towards me. Not having lived intimately with wild goats I did not know how belligerent she might be. There being no place for me to retreat to there remained only the exciting alternative of standing my ground to see what would take place.

She came on in a most determined manner, shaking her head threateningly and pawing the ground. It was difficult to keep her in focus as she approached. At sixteen feet she suddenly dropped to her knees, lowered her head, and tore up the heather and earth around its

45

roots, pitching them vehemently from side to side. Interesting, to be sure, but when would she decide enough was enough?

She was a spectacle of wild womanhood I shall never, never forget. Half of her heavy winter coat had been rubbed off, leaving a flying furry wrap of long stained hair from her midriff back. The wind fluffed this up in billowy folds about her form. The sun seemed to sharpen her dagger black horns until she was a sublime picture of a mountain demon who pawed the dust and flung it about her in wild abandon with flailing hooves.

Surely all of this was not a protest at my presence! Or was it? I was prepared for the worst. Then, with a long sigh, she subsided into a heap in her dust bath; started to munch her cud in sublime contentment, while her kid nestled down close by. The pair of them were surrounded with heather blossoms and alpine flowers.

Perfect serenity!

If ever there was an anti-climax this was one. I could scarcely credit what had taken place!

By this time another ewe and her kid, as well as a yearling, had emerged from the canyon and were dusting themselves. The late evening sun, too, was a tonic that they indulged in.

It was eight o'clock by the time I had exposed my last bit of film. I knew there was a long tricky trail back to my cache, but first for fun I inched up to see just how close I could come to my new acquaintances.

Moving forward as imperceptibly as I could I managed to get within six and a half feet of the nearest old girl. At this distance she suddenly felt I had taken sufficient liberties with her. She announced her disgust with a loud snort, bounded back from me and took her companions in a hair-raising plunge back down into the dark depths of the canyon where first I had found them.

Keyed up from the tenseness of the long 'freeze' I relaxed and wandered back along the trail. Sunlight tinted the rocks and vegetation in glowing grandeur. The stars blinked on in the darkness. That was one of the most soul-satisfying trails I ever tramped, for it was sweet with the fruit borne of repeated failure and now finally success.

7
Bold Billy and the Kid

AT VARIOUS times my luck in photographing mountain goats had been almost uncanny. One thing about it, however, that rather irked me was that in every encounter with these crafty animals I had met only nannies and kids.

One day my luck changed. It changed in such an unusual manner that I feel the tale is worth telling. At least it shows how exciting and unpredictable life in the high mountains can be.

It was late October in the northern Rockies. New snow was lying thick and soft over the Opal Hills. I had climbed up over them in search of caribou that sometimes frequented the little basin behind them.

There had been no caribou there since the snow came, for there were no tracks. The country was desolate and abandoned, apart from one lonely fox track that showed where he had flushed a ptarmigan from beneath the snow.

I was not dismayed by the barren landscape. It was mid-morning. The brittle blue shadows on the snow cast by the sharp sunlight made me content with the sweep and wonder of the white world about me. The keen air, the long views, the feeling of solitude and freedom urged me to push on along the face of a nearby mountain range.

The light unsettled snow covered loose scree and made progress across the steep slopes a treacherous game. More than once the jumbled stones worked loose under my weight. With a rumble they would start tumbling end over end, gathering snow and debris in their erratic bouncing course, into the yawning basins below. Only quick foot-work kept me from going with them. An hour of this found me perspiring freely, not only because of the exertion of maintaining my delicate balance on the treacherous slides, but also because of its pure thumping thrill.

Ahead of me I could see a broad high bench, which wind had scoured clean of snow, leaving it black and bare. Here I decided to rest. It seemed good to be able to walk upright and at ease again. Before sitting down I reconnoitred the fringe of snow just in case a stray animal had perchance passed that way.

To my delight I discovered immense goat tracks, fresh that morning and belonging to only one animal. 'But what would he be doing away up here this time of year?' I wondered to myself, feeling quite sure that only a lone Billy would be encountered in such a spot.

When the tracks appeared, my fatigue disappeared. With new zest I started off on the meandering trail that seemed to lead in no definite direction. Looking down continually at the glare of white that bounced from the surface of the snow I wondered if I would become blinded. To reduce the danger I shut my eyelids until only mere slits were left to let the bright light in. I knew this was the principle the Eskimos had used with their ancient whale-bone eye-shields that carried only a tiny slit to peer through.

The plan certainly reduced eye strain, but it also made my chances of seeing the old Billy, before he saw me, very much poorer. As it was he would be difficult enough to spot in his long white winter coat against these winter mountains.

Suddenly it seemed he bounded out from under my very feet. Actually I was not that close to him. Such surprises always leave one with the impression that the animal was closer than it really is. Just the same, the old rascal had been counting on his camouflage. He stood in a small draw without moving, hoping I would pass above him. But I had stuck to his trail and the ruse did not work.

With an awkward rocking-horse gait that managed to propel him rapidly through the snow and across deep drifts he was gone. I could hardly believe he had vanished so suddenly. Doubly determined I floundered along his trail until it emerged on to a sharp ragged rock ridge. Here he knew he would leave no tell-tale tracks. Momentarily my former weariness returned. By now it was afternoon and a bite of lunch would taste good. 'What's more I'll give him a little time to calm down,' I mused, looking for a spot where I could shelter from the rising wind.

Ensconced behind an overhanging cornice of snow on the leeward side of the ridge I unwrapped my sardines, rye crisp, and dried figs. Even the sardine oil was tempting and tasty in the cold biting air. Refreshed, I drank deeply of the glory of the high country that rolled away from my look-out in every direction. Range after range, peak piled on peak, all glistening in their sheaths of wind-polished ice. What a panorama! What a day to have lived!

With renewed hope I climbed to the crest of the rock ridge. I scanned its entire perimeter of snow for tracks. There were none. I retraced my steps and started to reconnoitre the ridge from where the goat tracks left off before. By great good luck I found where here and there he had stepped inadvertently on small patches of snow lodged in cracks and crevices.

I was startled to discover that he had made a complete about turn, doubled back on his tracks, and actually followed me when I went to look for shelter to eat my lunch. While I was busy with my rye crisp and sardines, the wily old fellow had stood on a small knoll, not more than sixty feet behind me, and watched me lunch, perhaps highly amused by my diet. He then returned to the rocks, and was now, as far as I could see, dissolved into the mountain whiteness.

Again I scanned all the snow encircling the rocks for his tracks. Still there were none. 'Then doggone his hide he must be somewhere around these rocks,' I muttered half defiantly.

A careful investigation of the jumbled outcrop on which I stood disclosed that it had an overhang to it. It suddenly occurred to me that perhaps he had secreted himself beneath this. I had once seen a nanny do this so effectively that I had never forgotten the trick. Gingerly I began to scramble about the broken rock and peer over. Directly below me I noticed a patch of white not quite as pure as the surrounding snow. It was the old Billy standing like a statue. I took a rather unimpressive photograph of the top of his back at 110 feet.

'Surely I can do better than this,' I thought, looking for a way down. By the most cautious manœuvring over loose boulders and snow patches, I eased myself down another twenty feet and got a little better perspective of the goat at ninety feet. He still had not detected my movements above him. I wondered what his fate might have been had I been a cougar. Yet most authorities claim goats have little to fear from even those cunning predators.

Congratulating myself on my climbing skill thus far, I decided to drop down to a ledge which appeared to be almost on a level with the old Billy. This proved a dangerous idea. After all I was alone in high remote country. One slip and a broken leg or crushed body would have found me freshly frozen in short order. But calculated risks are half the thrill of wildlife stalking. I felt my long dream of such a fine bold Billy in these wild surroundings merited the try.

At first I made marvellous progress without dislodging a stone or creating a stir that would alert the old devil. The ledge narrowed ominously as I wormed along it. The goat was coming into view now. I could see the wind playing in his long white whiskers. The shoe-black polish of his horns was lively.

Then there came a sickening sensation. I stepped on a patch of ice and it crumbled. In an instant I felt myself clawing at the rocks with my hands. My boots fought for footing as the ledge broke under my weight. With a rumble of rolling rock I slithered to a merciful halt on a precarious out-jut of granite. I can still recall how beautiful it looked to me at that moment—more for its rescue than for the rare red lichens adorning its surface.

The goat meanwhile was gone. Thunderstruck by my unexpected and noisy appearance he fled in panic. I have never seen any wild animal go quite so far, so fast against such tremendous obstacles. One moment he stood drowsily in his imagined sun-bathed sanctuary below the overhanging ridge. The next moment he was a terror-stricken bundle of flying fur that hurled himself down across the snowfields of the yawning valley below us.

Collecting my own wits I sat motionless on my dangerous perch and watched his flight. I was glad of the diversion from my own peril. I felt sure he would head all the way down the mountainside. He did not. Reaching the valley floor he immediately launched himself at the slope on the other side and started a tortuous trail towards the formidable peak that reared up to its 9,000-foot crown above us.

I pulled myself together and crawled back to the ledge from which I had come. It was the only way out. My heart was pounding from more than mere altitude. Gradually I wormed back along it and out on to broad safe footing.

All this time the old Billy pushed his way up and up and up. Through drifts, across broken ridges, over deep draws his climb was relentless. A rough guess was that he mounted a full two miles to finally disappear over the very summit. He was bold and brave, a tribute to his wild glorious domain.

Terribly tired but tremendously thrilled I turned from the sight and meandered down to lower valleys while the western sun turned the mountains to pure gold.

On the way down I encountered another band of goats. Amongst them was one mischievous youngster. He stood high, silvery white on the sword-like edge of a snow cornice that leaned sharply into the frank blue of the October sky. It was high, very lofty, remote and silent, this icy ridge in the northern Rockies. Its dazzling brightness of reflected light that bounced off the wind-polished surfaces of surrounding peaks seemed to transport it to heaven itself.

Yet there on the airy skyline stood this tiny particle of furry flesh and blood that bound the vista to solid soil. Peering out from the long dense wool were two bright, beady eyes—sparkling with devilment. Momentarily he paused on the lip of snow peering down at the deep bluish shadows that his own form shot across the steep golden slopes below him.

He had just laboured up that grade by pawing a trail strenuously through the deep white powder. Others of his kind laboured upward along the same route far beneath him. Suddenly in a flash of fun he dislodged a chunk of snow that tumbled over the edge. Fascinated, he watched it hurtle down the long mountainside past his pals.

I almost thought I could see him grin as it rolled to a stop on the valley floor. Nonchalantly he turned and moved on up the skyline, a white puff of wind-whipped fur.

A goat rolling snowballs on his playmates.

He was still just a kid!

8
Rocky Mountain Rams

A FINE ram's head is to many sportsmen in North America the ultimate achievement and noblest reward in the pursuit of big game.

This can be explained best by two very diverse reasons. The first being the sheer magnificence and monarch-like impression conveyed by a wild ram high up in his native haunts. This majestic creature is, in my estimation, rivalled only by a mature bull elk bugling his mating call in the high alpine meadows in the fall.

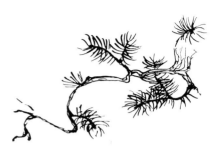

The other far more practical reason why sheep are so highly regarded is the hunting skill required to bag one. This does not mean that good heads are never secured by novices. They are, and 'beginners' luck' applies here as in most other fields. On the other hand to hunt for the crafty old monarchs generally entails long climbs, stalking skill, alert eyes, good wind, and rugged endurance.

It can be understood, then, why it was with some trepidation that I made my first trip into the Rockies to photograph these beautiful animals. Fortunately more than a fair share of 'beginners' luck' came my way. Had it not, this chapter might well have been nothing more than a recital of long scrambles over high peaks, weary legs and frustrated feelings at being outwitted by the keen eyes and hardy stamina of the Bighorns.

October had been selected for the trip. The flocks would be moving down to lower elevations, driven by deep early snow that covered the summer ranges. Engrossed with gathering up their ewes before mating, the rams, I felt, would be more preoccupied than usual and thus afford me a better opportunity for stalking.

My first sight of Bighorns was a let down. It was late afternoon. The valley I was hunting was in shadow. Its slopes were bare and brown from summer sun and ghastly over-grazing. Suddenly, through the binoculars, I spotted moving shapes of an almost identical shade nibbling their way across the sombre scene.

By working up through a draw garnished with the tumbling leaves of trembling aspens I was startled to find a band of thin, ragged ewes and their curious lambs at the forest edge.

'Worms!' That was the first thought that leaped into my mind. From their dull coats and unkempt appearance it was obvious that the sheep must have been infested with parasites.

This was not altogether surprising from the look of the range that had carried too many for too long. A severe disease epidemic or a vicious winter could very quickly decimate these poor flocks. Then, and only then, would the grass have a chance to reseed and re-establish itself over the gnawed ground. Or perhaps in their own innate wisdom the sheep would migrate to other mountain pastures. I hoped so.

This thought of their migrating was a pleasant one, but from knowledge of domestic sheep for many years, I knew not a very practical hope. These animals have a deeply ingrained affinity for particular bits of range. Wild sheep were no different. Though driven from favourite spots by predators, hunters, or even hunger, they will, in a very short time, return to the same mountain, basin, or ridge which is 'home'.

Working my way cautiously through the aspens that evening, it surprised me to find a fair sprinkling of young rams among the ewes. But not a single mature 'battler' was in sight.

Because of the poor light the only alternative left to me was to try and photograph the ewes on the skyline against the western light in silhouette. This involved crawling and creeping on my stomach along their little sheep paths, attempting to get within range.

One thing I learned very quickly was that their alertness was directly proportional to the angle which I was below them. If directly beneath they showed little fear. As their own level was reached they became increasingly uneasy. To be above them meant flight and failure every time.

Something that struck me at once was the immense patch of white on the rump, bisected by a thin dark line terminating in the black tail. Again and again I have pondered why so many wild animals have a tendency towards this pattern of accenting the stern with light markings.

To name but a few, it applies to sheep, elk, deer, and rabbits on this continent, while in Africa the Grant's gazelle, Thompson's gazelle, waterbuck, and impala are all adorned with some white pattern on the rump.

The explanation given to me as a child was always that, in flight, this served as a 'flag' the young could follow readily through the bush. In part this may apply. Yet there must be a deeper design than that. Camouflage may be a partial purpose. A bright reflecting surface that discourages insects about the rectum may be another. Each fits under certain conditions. None holds throughout.

That first evening the unsatisfactory light, the discouraging sight of poor animals, and the absence of mature rams left me in a bleak mood. This was not helped by rain which made my camp by the river that night a wretched affair. Cold fall rains in the mountains can be sheer torture, especially when everything freezes up and a tent crackles like a plastic bag sheathed in ice.

55

The next morning broke clear like cut glass. By daybreak I was back up on the sheep range for I knew how fickle the mountain weather could be, and every hour of bright sunshine was to be cherished for camera work. Here all the elements of superb pictures were present: wild game, fresh snow on the peaks, and bright sun. Now to combine them!

Just as the rays of sunshine pierced the clear air, so did sound have the ability to penetrate long distances through the still clean atmosphere. That was why the very first sound I heard as I toiled up the steep slope was the distant crash of horn on horn.

It was among the most thrilling sensations to have come my way in a life full of wilderness experiences. There would be a pause, then the heavy thudding shock would reverberate down the slope to where I struggled upwards. My imagination was aglow with the thought of the giant rams in deadly combat. These were big rams—no mistake.

When I neared the crest of the ridge the sound of head crashing against head subsided. I had not seen the combatants, but perhaps they had spotted me.

Flat on my stomach, inching ahead, my face buried deep under a thick wool cap to conceal it, I peered over the edge and almost fainted.

Not over eighty feet away stood four of the most imposing lords of the wilderness I shall ever hope to see. They stood there, broadside to me in a group, their mighty heads together like bronze statues reflecting the golden sunlight.

Imagine all this with their pedestal the knife edge of a mountain ridge that dropped away into the dark blue depths of a valley, while beyond and behind their glistening bodies stood range on range of snowy heights.

I do not feel ashamed to admit here that this superb sight moved me deeply. There was, in the natural dignity of these splendid rams, a grandeur of wild glory that human language cannot portray.

Only those who know the far flung freedom of high untamed country, of which the Bighorns are such a regal part, can grasp the sensations that swept over me in those introductory seconds.

Collecting myself, I slowly, ever so slowly, moved the camera to my eye and took a shot just as they started to disband. Later in the day, after they had become adjusted to my presence on their range, I was able to secure quite attractive photographs of them, both active and in repose, with the ewes and lambs.

Reliving those moments by my camp-fire that night I reflected on the stages of transition through which a person passes who spends much time with wildlife. It might be almost called a form of growth or metamorphosis.

In early childhood there is that simple desire to capture and hold in the hand the beetle, frog, or butterfly that passes our way. This gives place to the boyhood concept of acquiring skill with a slingshot, bow and arrow, or a rifle, using animals and birds as targets. In turn this is overshadowed by the pursuit of game and pride of adolescence in the size and quantity of kill.

With the passage of time and maturity of mind, men find even deeper satisfaction in the sheer thrill of the stalk, the out-of-doors, the sight of wildlife, a record head.

In an attempt to convey these experiences to others and to preserve them in something of a tangible form, some of us have left behind the rifle and shotgun, substituting the camera—a step that calls for even greater bush craft, more endurance, cunning, patience, and a passionate love for the game.

With all of this there remain episodes in one's wilderness experiences that are never reproduced on film; that no words will ever adequately represent. Thus the ultimate heights to which we mortals can aspire in dealing with wildlife in its native haunts is that indescribable pleasure of going to the mountains, woods, plains, or rivers with an open heart and mind. There to allow Nature herself to inscribe her own winsomeness indelibly on our lives as we linger quietly before her.

That precisely was what I attempted to do that glorious October day high in the Rockies in company with this band of sheep. The mere acquisition of pictures was secondary. The profound panorama etched on my memory by those surroundings is a masterpiece, one of a large art collection that cannot be bought or sold at any price.

By far the greatest impact made on the mind by these sheep is, of course, the massive horns on the rams. In very old ones the girth at the base is immense. The horns may be chipped from battle, and the tips 'broomed' by continuous rubbing on rocks to keep the points from growing into and thus obstructing the line of vision.

The size of horn varies from region to region. For example sheep on limestone-rich mountains appear invariably to possess heavier horns than those in areas deficient in calcium, which is to be expected.

This entire field of soils, their mineral content, vegetative cover, and consequent influence on wildlife populations is a fascinating study.

It is my conviction that many of the subdivisions of species which biologists appear to delight in, would not be necessary if an entire group of animals were viewed in the light of the total environment which they reflected.

An instance of this is the arbitrary division between the West Coast Columbia Black Tail deer and the Mule deer of the Interior mountains. The two deer interbreed indiscriminately. Apart from size and minute differences in colouration they are identical. My own observation would be that in the calcium deficient coastal areas with their impoverished, rain-leached soils, the Black Tail deer cannot hope to attain maximum scale. In the dry interior with the highly mineralized soils rich in calcium and phosphates the same animal acquires the size and scale of a Mule deer.

On the coast it is common for deer to frequent the sea shore where trace minerals can be picked up from eating seaweed and licking dried salt water deposits off the rocks. Nevertheless, this does not compensate for the continuous mineral lack in their vegetative diet.

Even the deer and sheep of the Rockies I noticed were fond of the mineral licks, some of which had obviously been used for hundreds of years. One, I remember especially, had a fir tree growing in the centre of it. The gradual licking and nibbling of innumerable little tongues and lips had removed all the soil from around the main roots to a depth of three or four feet, so that the tree looked comical as though standing on tall stilts. To support itself other roots had been sent out laterally which in turn were gradually undermined, giving it the appearance of being supported in space by aerial roots.

Strangely enough it is in the spring of the year that the sheep frequent these licks the most. It is as though they need a 'spring tonic' to tone up their bodies after the meagre fare and long hardships of the winter. It also fits the ewes for lambing time.

Actually the very first flush of tender green growth in the spring though eaten eagerly by animals, is low in nutritive value, and they sometimes expend more energy in searching for it than the grass provides. Coupled with this is its extreme laxative effect, consequently many of the weaker specimens actually succumb in the spring after having survived the winter. This also accounts for their use of the licks at this crucial period.

Another habit that interested me was the frequency and amount of water which they drank. Domestic sheep will scorn water if there is rain or dew on their grazing. This obviously did not apply to the wild ones I observed in the Rockies. Even though it rained or snowed practically every day, they visited the river to drink each afternoon— and drank deeply.

One evening a young lamb astounded me by drinking avidly from a small muddy pool of rain water that had accumulated in a depression lying in one of their sheep trails. A thing that I would not have believed unless I had seen it with my own eyes.

The behaviour of the lambs generally was most entertaining. The affection they showed for the oldest rams intrigued me. They would nuzzle the old boys under the chin and neck while the latter closed their eyes in blissful contentment with upraised muzzle.

Their agility, too, while perhaps not as spectacular as the mountain goat, certainly commands respect. Their short, rather sturdy, bodies belied the nimble agility of their strong muscles. With ease they could make a vertical leap several times their own height from a standing position. At dusk they indulged in all the racing, chasing, climbing, and clowning common to their kind.

The ewes were a gentle lot, content to be herded and escorted by their big-horned lords, but ever alert to any new danger that lurked in their beloved mountains.

It is frequently small, unspectacular observations with wild creatures that prove the most rewarding. Certainly this has been true in my experience. I will come home from a day in the field with perhaps nothing more for my efforts than one insignificant little fresh discovery about the life habits of wild creatures. Yet that is enough to have made the day utterly worthwhile.

Several simple examples with wild sheep will show what I mean. I had gone into a mountain range looking for a small band of California Big Horns. This was broken, fragmented sandstone country with a fresh fall of snow dappling the brown rocks.

59

I worked up into a small sun-drenched basin. I felt sure the sheep would linger here to gain what relief they could from the cold snap that had suddenly plunged the early fall temperatures to zero. It was an ideal sheep range with patches of dry bunch grass now brown with frost, scattered among the boulders and benches of rock. The wind had drifted the snow around the range, but also swept bare spots where the ewes and rams would come to feed.

With my binoculars I combed the country but it seemed empty. A second time I went over it without success. My sense of wild animal behaviour was insistent, however, and I was positive there must be sheep in the basin.

My hunch was confirmed a few moments later when I spotted a dun object moving among the rocks. It was a young ram! So perfectly camouflaged was he that had there been no movement I would never have spotted him. But the reason for this was not only because the brown body blended with the brown stones, but also because of the white rump patch which matched so beautifully the dabs of snow amongst the rocks.

Earlier I have remarked on this curious marking of wild animals which carry a distinct white rump patch. This particular morning, its great usefulness for sheep was proven to me beyond a shadow of doubt. To my amazement the camouflage was so perfect that it was uncanny.

Another careful scrutiny disclosed no other sheep than this ram. I decided to stalk him, happy in the thought that since he was alone this would offer far less difficulty than attempting to crawl up on an entire band.

I had scarcely moved a hundred yards when a magpie fluttered about noisily near the ram. The bird shrieked his alarm and I wondered if the cunning rascal had detected me even before the ram.

I focussed the glasses on the sheep again and was non-plussed to see not one animal but three. Two ewes that had been standing perfectly still beside the ram seemed to come to life out of the mottled background of rock and snow.

This was a strange sensation to describe. But it was even more humiliating a moment later when a fourth object moved. What had passed as a boulder a moment earlier took on the flesh and form of the most magnificent mountain sheep I ever laid eyes upon. I have always been credited with unusual eyesight for detecting animals, but the perfect blending of these four sheep mocked me and made me realize how far I had been surpassed.

The view of the big ram was a blood warming experience. The cunning monarch had obviously seen me ever since I entered the basin. He knew his best defence was to stand still. So did the ewes. Only the movement of the inexperienced yearling had given them away. Otherwise I might have departed confident that there had been no sheep in the country.

Since my earlier hopes of getting within camera range easily were now shattered in the presence of the crafty old ram I decided to sit down a while and allow them to adjust to my presence. So I sat and studied them through the binoculars.

To my astonishment I saw the magpie return and fly down to alight on the back of one of the ewes. The sheep accepted the bird with obvious pleasure. She laid back her ears, relaxed her eyes and started to chew her cud as the bird combed her body with its beak.

Oftentimes I had watched cowbirds do this to cattle and sheep on the ranch. Of course, too, it was a common sight with tick birds in Africa, that lived off the parasites found on both domestic and wild animals. Yet this was the first time I ever saw magpies act in this capacity.

The old ewe relished the attention lavished on her by the big black-and-white bird. She allowed him to crawl all over her head, neck and even between her legs and under her belly. The first job completed, the magpie then flew to the second ewe and was joined by a second bird before finally departing.

Perhaps the rams got their ideas from the birds. Anyway, it intrigued me to see how they would walk up side by side and start to nuzzle and comb each other's flanks and shoulders with their teeth. This they did with great gusto and relish. It amused me to see how a ram would contort his head and neck to enable his benefactor to reach every crevice and corner of his anatomy. I cannot be sure whether this manicure only removed ticks, keds, and the accumulated salty skin flakes from a sheep's body or whether it also serves some other useful purpose in conditioning the hide and hair.

Presently the sheep seemed satisfied with their toilet and moved off to feed. For the balance of the day I moved with them, climbing to increasingly formidable peaks and crags.

It was here that I learned that these nimble-footed mountaineers find ice and snow-covered rocks distasteful. The old ram launched himself at one ledge sheathed in sparkling, glassy ice that broke away and tinkled down below his weight. When he crashed back and landed on the rocks below he was unnerved. Turning quickly he plunged away from the treacherous surface, found sure footing on a more gradual incline, and led the band bounding down a steep ravine into deep timber.

Even though I have frequently
met with mountain sheep in
timbered country,
somehow they are always associated
in my mind with
the high ridges and rock ramparts
of our great mountains.
There they are a majestic part
of our wilderness glory.

THE RAMPARTS

EDGE OF THE SILVER FOREST

MY MOUNTAIN LAKE

PILEATED WOODPECKER

LOOKOUT

WHITE RAM

A SPIKE IN THE VELVET

MY FRIEND

COTTON GRASS ON ALPINE LAKE

COYOTE LISTENING

YELLOW BELLIED MARMOTS

THE BUGLER

LONE RAM

CANADA GEESE WITH GOSLINGS

SUNNING HIMSELF

WINTER SNOW

CANADA JAY

THE RAMPARTS

BULL MOOSE WADING

GAME TRAIL

GOLDEN MANTLED
GROUND SQUIRREL

A BULL ELK AND HIS HAREM

RAM

BEAVER HOUSE AND POND

HOARY MARMOT

FALL FOLIAGE

IT'S JUST ME

9
Feeble Folk

ANYONE who has spent much time in our northern mountains will, I think, agree that much of their charm is provided by the small animals which make their home in the high country.

It is not uncommon to make expeditions into the back country without seeing big game. After my life in Africa's big-game country this fact never has ceased to arouse my wonderment. In East Africa if one did not see elephants, buffalo, rhino, or lion, at least there would always be a few scattered plains animals about. Or if one was in the bush country or forests, creatures such as duiker, monkeys, or wild pigs were encountered often enough to make most safaris lively and full of interest.

In the North American wilderness this simply is not the case. One photographic expedition in particular which I made demonstrated beyond any doubt just how destitute of wildlife a region can be at times. During a period of five full days I consistently averaged hiking twenty miles a day, always travelling with the utmost caution and at the same time scanning all the surrounding country. Yet I failed to see a solitary creature larger than a coyote the entire time.

Now this was in a region ordinarily frequented by grizzly bears, caribou, moose, mule deer, cougars, and wolves. I found tracks and signs of all the above species without once setting eyes on the owners.

It is during these barren periods that the photographer or hiker turns to the lesser creatures for comfort and companionship. The more one stops to study them the more fascinating do they become. On the other hand even to the casual visitor the mountains assume a deeper dimension in their memory because of that shrill piercing whistle that a marmot sends rocketing across the upland basin, bouncing from rock to rock in its echo.

Nor can the fresh tracks of a varying hare fleeing across the snow from his pursuer help but give a fleeting thrill to anyone who comes across them on the trail.

It is fitting, then, that in a book of this sort, brief mention of these little folk should be made. They have enriched my days on the trail. They have added great pleasure to hours in camp, and they have provided a challenge all of their own in attempting to photograph them in their wild retreats.

Among my favourites is the hoary marmot or 'whistler' as he is so appropriately nicknamed. His close relatives are the 'yellow-bellied' marmots of lower levels and the ground hogs or woodchuck of plain and farmland.

The 'whistler' is to be met with only three or four months in the year. This is when the summer sun has removed the white covers from his high wild country and dressed the meadows in the rich abundance of alpine plants and grasses which are his favourite fare.

There he gorges himself on the fresh green succulents until his hoary hide is full of fat. With the advent of autumn frosts that sear the foliage brown, he retreats deep into the sanctuary of his rock-bound lair to sleep away the next eight or nine months. A lazy life to be sure, yet an existence fraught with fear.

The fearful portion is that of summertime. It is then that the bears are abroad with their young, hungry for meat to fortify themselves and produce the rich milk craved by their cubs. Marmots are their dainty dish and the big brutes will go to incredible toil and feats of strength in tearing open the rock dens to reach the 'whistlers'.

The marmot's whistle of alarm when a bear is about and bent on such tactics, is a continuous series of short, sharp staccato 'beeps' almost identical to the wireless time signal of the B.B.C. Nor will the cry relent until the bear has left for good.

If it is a man, eagle, coyote, or hawk who may suddenly have invaded the whistler's tranquil domain, the alarm is a long piercing note that rings across the valley. It will be picked up by others scattered about on their favourite rock piles. Then the sound will go winging on the wind, echoing and re-echoing across the heights; one of the finest wild calls of the wilderness.

Perhaps it is because of my affection for them that I have given as much time as I have to studying and photographing these animals. In any event some of my happiest hours have been spent watching them with their families playing about the boulders, sunning themselves and feeding amid the flowers.

There are few places indeed in the mountains where the marmot is not met with. With the peca or cony this is not true, for these little fellows have a most irregular distribution in our high country. In one area they will abound, the next there will be none.

Nor, like the marmot, does this tiny creature go into a long winter sleep. Quite the opposite, he appears to be active most of the year round. I have been astounded to hear his faint warning notes of 'ee-ee-ee' coming up from his rocky bedroom through several feet of snow when my footsteps on the crust announced a stranger.

Instead of laying up a layer of fat against winter chill, the peca prefers to store up piles of cut grass, herbs, and leaves which are his hay. This material is hoarded in hollows between boulders where it is accessible under the snow and serves to keep his internal fires fueled through the long dark months.

The cony is an attractive little bundle of fur with a mouse-like face surmounted by two large rounded ears from which protrude a fine fringe of conspicuous hairs. Because of his minute size, but wise choice of a rock-girt home, he has little to fear from bears who would not deem one mouthful of peca worth the rock work to get him.

It is not that bears disdain small morsels of meat. It is simply that they must comply with the law of diminishing returns whereby it would be foolish to expend more strength to acquire this meat than it could possibly make up for.

Proof of this lies in the time, though less strenuous effort, bears will put into collecting mice. To watch a huge grizzly, perhaps nearly 1,000 pounds in weight, running his comb-like claws through the dry grass to collect mice is almost comical.

Mice, of course, come in almost as many shades and sub-species as there are colours in the rainbow. This is fortunate since they form one of the great foundation supplies of food for a wide array of birds and mammals. From grizzly bears to sparrow hawks a large segment of the entire North American fauna rests in part on the prolificacy of mice.

So, when I think of mice it is not in terms of dirty brown nuisances nibbling the cheese in my pantry, or chewing circles in closet doors. Rather I like to think of them as I have met them in my camps in the forest or on the ridges.

One of the commonest and certainly most adorable members of this family are our little white-footed mice. With their soft grey backs and downy white underparts they are distinctly pretty creatures. Their comparative lack of fear for man gives them a cheeky familiarity that is quite fascinating.

One early morning when I went to get some minerals, that I had stored in an ancient iron kettle, for my sheep, I was amused to find it full of four, fat, white-footed mice. One of them ran up the spout and squeezed his jelly-like form out of the mouth with a funny little shiver that almost made you think of warm grey water bubbling out.

These mice are as much at home in the trees as on the ground in the forest. One of their favourite pastimes is to scurry along through the lower limbs as though playing follow the leader with each other. These games have often taken them over my tent, across my sleeping-bag, and even through my hair.

One camp in particular that I had on the Athabaska River in the Rockies was notorious for mice nights. With the moon shining full on the semi-transparent tent I would lie in my bag and watch them race up the tent ropes, climb to the ridge pole, then slide and scurry down the sides, like skiers elated over a fresh fall of snow on a slope.

Two rather remarkable characteristics of these mice is that they are known to frequent the highest elevations of any mammals (15,000–16,000 feet) on the mountains of North America. The other is that they have a frail, bird-like song which is not generally thought of as coming from a mouse.

Another camp I recall vividly because of mice was one where I had chosen to sleep right beside a trout stream. The first part of the night was occupied with listening to bears splashing about in the water after fish. When they had finally found other interests and I was dozing off to sleep a band of mice decided to hold a dance on my sleeping-bag. I had no tent to amuse them this time.

I did not begrudge them this fun for the first few minutes. In fact I was rather intrigued with the sensation of their tiny feet racing over the khaki covers. When the game continued I decided sleep was more important for the stiff climb the next day so I would toss the covers, sending the wee rascals for an unexpected flight. Several treatments of this sort ensured slumber for the rest of the night.

Whereas mice are nocturnal in habit, the chipmunks and ground squirrels move about by day. Next to the marmots, my best friends are these cheerful striped individuals who race through the under-growth and chirp so gaily in their travels. Even the most drab setting takes on warmth and life the moment a chipmunk appears.

Their swift erratic movements almost exceed the eyes' ability to follow them. It is this rollicking sense of dash and verve that endears them so.

One mountain trip I made with a companion who became very ill during our second day out. By great good fortune we had a log cabin in which he could rest. The surroundings of this cabin though attractive with meadows and woodland were utterly bereft of wildlife. I rather

suspected that the cabin's previous occupants had amused themselves by shooting everything that walked or flew within sight of the camp; so that by the time we arrived it had acquired the complexion of a morgue.

Oddly enough the only bright memory of that lifeless camp which lingers in mind is the swift scurrying of a chipmunk who had his headquarters in a juniper thicket back of the log cabin. It must have been that his restless energy had saved his life from the 'trigger happy' shooters. It pleased me to think that he had outdone them. A sly satisfaction creeps into my heart when I think of the chagrin their misses must have caused. If curses could have killed, the wee chap would certainly have succumbed long ago.

Instead there he was, darting about almost as swift as a deer fly. As my companion recovered his strength he would sit on a block of firewood by the door in the afternoon sunshine and try to photograph the blur of fur that raced about in the bushes. It would have been hard to discover a more effective tonic—it was such an absorbing game he soon forgot his ills.

Chipmunks can live without any water except the dew. Even out in the bare sagebrush country of the interior their numbers are enormous. They dash through the sagebrush, out into the trails, and through the dry grass with feverish frenzy. Even when harvesting grass, seeds, or berries they seem to act as though time was precious and not a minute dare be wasted as they pack their cheek pouches with rapidity.

It is hard to believe that these tiny creatures can push as many as 300 oat kernels into their elastic pouches in one single trip. Loaded to capacity they dash off to cache the crops and come flying back for more.

In the more northerly sections, the chipmunk shares his habitat with our varying hares. In the sagebrush country it is the jack rabbit and in the lower country the common cotton-tail.

I must confess that my encounters with rabbits in high country have been remarkably few and far between.

The distribution of rabbits in the north-west country is an absorbing study. For example there are no native wild rabbits on Vancouver Island. The gulf islands between Vancouver Island and the mainland carry a substantial rabbit population of mixed origin.

In the north country the numbers of rabbits from year to year fluctuate tremendously. Definite cycles have been established wherein over a seven-to-ten-year period the number of rabbits pyramids to a colossal peak, then suddenly the species is practically wiped out. It must then build up again from a few surviving individuals. The precise causes of this fluctuation are not known, although disease and lack of suitable feed from overcrowding undoubtedly play a part.

Since a number of northern fur-bearing animals, especially lynx, wolverine, and foxes, depend on them for food, their numbers, too, fluctuate with the cycle of the rabbits.

Like the ptarmigan of the north, our varying hares turn pure white in winter, then back to brown for summer. Although seldom seen, at least their tracks have always intrigued me, for by following their etching in the snow it is possible to revive the drama of the night before.

Out on the Pacific coast, where rain rather than snow is the rule in winter, the varying hare retains his brown coat all the year round. This is one of the most outstanding examples of which I know whereby a species has adapted itself to a particular environment.

One dawn in the Rockies, just as I was stirring from my sleeping-bag, I could hear the thud-thud-thud of approaching feet on the run. A terror-stricken rabbit in full flight passed within a few inches of my head oblivious of my presence. Seconds later another runner could be heard coming. This was a coyote who was startled by my sudden appearance from the ground.

Another day I watched a hawk attempting to capture a rabbit on a grassy hilltop. The bird's sharp eyes had detected the rabbit lying in his 'form' inside a small patch of brush. His dive miscarried and the startled rabbit rushed out from under the outstretched talons. The bird took a few seconds to regain altitude before taking another dive at the fleeing quarry. The rabbit made a sudden turn at top speed and eluded his attacker again.

These tactics were repeated at least half a dozen times. It seemed to me that the rabbit was doomed for lack of adequate cover. Gradually he had circled in his zig-zag course until he was almost back at his form. A devilish plunge by the hawk struck him, knocking him sideways, but again the talons did not go home. I could only guess it was an immature bird not yet fully skilled in hunting.

After this the terror-stricken rabbit reached the safety of a small clump of bushes; the hawk, who had lost the advantage after his last fumble, climbed back up into the blue a disappointed hunter.

Somehow it had never occurred to me that these timid creatures had a chance to survive except through mere fecundity. Now I know better, for the odds certainly had been very much against this one who had shown a great will to live!

One of the feeble folk who can prove formidable on occasion is the common porcupine. This is a slow-moving creature who appears to move only with great deliberation.

My first encounter with one proved a painful experience for the dog that was with me. He was eager for combat and ended up with about twenty of the devilish quills anchored in his mouth and jaws.

The fact that the quills have minute barbs on them make it exceedingly difficult to pull them out except with a strong pair of pliers. This is a painful procedure, but unless done the quills work deeper and deeper into the flesh.

81

Some hunters have found cougars and fisher with many of the quills embedded in their flesh. The fisher especially makes a habit of killing porcupines either by rolling them on their backs so that the under side, bare of spines, can be ripped open or by finding them up in a tree where the slender trunk does not protect the entire stomach and it can be slashed from one side.

Porcupines can do a great deal of damage to a stand of trees in which they decide to feed. They girdle the trunk and cut off the flow of sap with the result that the tree either dies completely or is seriously stunted in growth.

They are solitary creatures and seldom encountered on the trail since they are nocturnal in habit. But where one travels in the forest their work can be seen. Nor is their trail in snow or dust an uncommon sight.

Occasionally their appetite for salt will lead them to chew on camp gear, tools, or any other articles that have come in contact with the salty taste of human hands or body perspiration. In fact one night I was startled to wake up and find one of these individuals clambering around on top of my sleeping-bag.

Since they are such slow creatures and so readily killed for food, they have been looked upon in Canada as a form of insurance for desperate winter travellers.

I have never eaten the flesh, but I am told that it is excellent in quality. This is not surprising since they live almost exclusively on vegetable matter—mainly bark and leaves.

Strange to say, generally only one or at the most two young ones are born at a time, and these tiny ones, virtually fully quilled at birth, may weigh as much as one pound, proving twice as large as bear cubs.

The largest porcupine I ever saw must have weighed close to twenty-five pounds. I had to shoot her because she persisted in returning every winter to girdle and damage a group of very choice pines that grew in one of my favourite valleys.

She proved quite a cunning creature, returning each night to den up in the cleft of a granite cliff that was virtually unassailable. Finally one morning after a fresh fall of snow I tracked her to her fortress by a route that I never knew existed.

It was a rather breath-taking climb that entailed descending a rock chimney to where a gigantic boulder had lodged in a crevasse. Rubble and debris had accumulated around this 'plug' and formed a veritable rock fort in which the porcupine had found a formidable retreat.

To reach it I had some ticklish climbing to do. By manœuvreing into a position from which I could look directly up into the den I discovered I could get a clear shot at her from below. However, the dilemma was how to keep clear myself when she tumbled out directly on top of me. I had merely wedged myself in the chimney with feet and shoulders so if her spiny body struck me full force it could well be enough to dislodge my hold, and I would go tumbling several hundred feet down the bluff with her.

Finally I spreadeagled myself between the rock walls. A clean shot brought her plunging down between my legs. That marked the reprieve for a bit of charming forest that would have died that winter under her gnawing teeth.

Some authorities feel we have protected porcupines too long to the serious detriment of some fine forest. I for one am inclined to agree, yet they do play their part and are most certainly a unique feature of our Canadian scene.

Again I repeat that were it not for the life and language of these feeble folk in our 'back' country, many trips there would be much less exciting than they are. What is more, often it is just because there are marmots, mice, chipmunks, or rabbits in an area that we are lucky enough to encounter bigger game who have come in search of them.

One of these, who himself is really not a very large animal, is the common coyote. Because this clever little gentleman is such a colourful character he merits mention here.

Just as the shrill whistle of the hoary marmot spells the voice of the remote lofty ridges, so does the plaintive cry of the coyote reveal the lonely spirit of the open plains, rangeland, and grassy meadows of the upper country.

So widespread and adaptable is this 'little wolf', as he is sometimes called, that his kind have spread themselves from seashore to snowline; from the eastern verges of the prairies to the warm shores of the Pacific; from the frigid fringes of the far north to the desperate deserts of Mexico.

Because of this, one is likely to encounter him almost anywhere that back trails lead into remote country. More often than not the only

83

indication that the cunning creature is about is the sharp staccato barking that trails off into a quavering wail. For me this unique and plaintive call carries within it the ring of wild places and wild country, for that is always where I have tingled in response to its sound.

Yet, unlike the great grey timber wolf, the coyote is not a creature to shun the haunts and homes of men. Quite the reverse, he has in fact fattened on the flocks of sheepmen, raided the runs of poultrymen, and generally outwitted the human race sufficiently to have survived in spite of the most ardent persecution.

His ability to survive is founded largely on his wit and his fecundity. Coyotes possess a native intelligence and cunning quite beyond that normally associated with lower creatures. I read a most intriguing book years ago written by a man who had spent a goodly portion of his life trying to outsmart coyotes as a predator hunter. Some of his accounts were almost uncanny in disclosing the sagacity of these furtive creatures.

I recall watching a pair hunting mice in the tall grass one day. I sat on a slope high above the grassy glade where they were busy in their partnership. I call it that because of the way the two co-operated in their work.

One would stand silently at the edge of the grass while the other pounced and drove the mice towards him to be snatched up unexpectedly. When satisfied with several such morsels they would trade places and the hunter would then have his turn to partake of the feast, which neither one could have achieved as readily alone.

The coyote does not, of course, confine his efforts in life only to rodents and smaller game. I stood entranced one evening on a high ridge in the Cascades and watched seven coyotes encircle two black tail does and their fawns in an open glade.

The coyotes had closed in a threatening circle around the four deer until only an area some fifty yards in diameter enclosed what I was sure to be a circle of death. First a coyote from one side, then the other alternately, would rush in and make a feinting attack on one of the deer. To my amazement the does displayed tremendous courage and cunning by retaliating with their sharp lightning charges, striking out viciously with cutting hooves.

I presumed the seven coyotes were all members of one family for this species does not normally hunt in packs as do wolves. Several of the coyotes appeared larger than the others, these I took to be the parents. It was not surprising to see so many young in a family, since at times as many as twelve pups will be born in a single litter. It is this fecundity which helps the coyote in his struggle for survival, as was so abundantly clear on this particular occasion.

After watching the uneven match for a while I sensed that the deer were tiring. The relentless whirling, dashing, charging tactics were

exhausting the does and any minute they would drop with utter fatigue or be quickly hamstrung.

Perhaps I should have checked myself to watch the ultimate outcome. I could not. My sympathies are always so strongly with the under-dog that in spite of myself I rushed down the hill whooping like an Indian. In an instant the battle was broken up and the deer were saved for another day.

The coyote on this continent is not altogether unlike the hyena of Africa in several respects. Both have the haunting cry that so epitomizes their native land; both are inclined to snoop and scavenge around human habitations; both take a terrible toll of the young from other species. But there the similarity ends.

To his credit the coyote consumes staggering numbers of rodents. Actually the important role played by the coyote in controlling rabbits, gophers, ground hogs, and mice of every description was not fully appreciated until his kind had almost been wiped out in some areas. Now one may travel over that same territory and encounter signs which read: 'NO HUNTING—COYOTES PROTECTED'. Once again we have had to learn that a species we despised had an important part in the over-all picture of our wildlife economy, which if we throw it far enough off balance, can very readily upset our own economy.

A graphic demonstration of this very point occurred two winters ago. Coyote numbers over much of Alberta's farming country were at an all-time low because of such a prolonged and efficient poisoning campaign directed against them. Then fall snow came early and buried a goodly portion of the grain crop which could not be harvested until spring.

Because there had been fewer coyotes, mice populations on the prairies had flourished. Then with an abundant banquet of grain under the snow to fortify their members it was natural that a veritable mice explosion took place. The loss in grain undoubtedly ran to many millions of dollars, and far exceeded the nominal damage done by coyotes in former years. No wonder prairie farmers are beginning to look on the little 'brush wolf' with a more benevolent eye. In fact it would not startle me some day to see signs erected along the fences of some farms which read: 'COYOTES WELCOME'—if only coyotes could read.

Annoying, useful, destructive, cunning, daring, deceptive, and even brash; the coyote is all of these. For me, however, he is the eternal romanticist of our great open spaces. I would feel poorer indeed if I had not been awakened at day dawn by his cry flinging itself from crag to crag across a desert canyon. I would have missed much of the melancholy mood of our mountains if I had never sat under a full moon and listened to that long wavering voice glance from the snowy slope of an upland meadow to go trembling down in quivering notes across the wild valleys of his wide domain.

10
Busy Beavers

To anyone who is familiar with our forests few things in nature can equal the rich sensations of pleasure and interest that signs of beaver industry arouse.

For a very long time my favourite walking-stick was a neatly chewed off alder sapling I had found along a beaver stream on northern Vancouver Island. It carried on it the sharp chisel marks of the beaver's teeth, which were singularly decorative.

Nor will I ever forget the first time I stumbled on a freshly cut poplar stump high in the Alberta foothills. From my earliest childhood I had read of the beavers' work and brooded over pictures of them, but in Africa they had no exact counterpart. So it was not until I was in my early twenties that I found this real honest-to-goodness beaver works.

The sight of the bright yellow wood gnawed the night before so entranced me that I immediately set out to explore the entire surrounding country for the dam, house, ponds, canals, slides, and other industrial developments that I had always associated with these retiring creatures.

Imagine my chagrin to find none of them. Only here and there odd bits and pieces of twigs and sticks stuck under a mud-bank. For, although I did not know it then, these were a family of bank beaver. At any rate failure to find their home did not discourage me from coming back that evening to lie in wait the whole night through, hoping to catch a glimpse of the wily rascals cutting down the poplars. They never did show up.

In fact it was not until many years later that I had a first-hand opportunity to watch these entertaining creatures busy about their business in the marshes. During all that time my interest in them never waned. Books by men like Grey Owl, who wrote so movingly of his life with beavers, left no doubt in my mind that they were creatures of amazing instincts and intelligence. For that reason I vowed a day would come when I would watch them for myself.

My heart literally skipped a beat one night, when, just at dusk, while walking back through the darkness to my camp, I noticed a whitish object at the edge of a forest clearing. My curiosity aroused I went over and there I discovered a fresh beaver stump, then another and another and another.

From the size of the trees and evidence of work all about I knew I had stumbled on a major operation. On the spot I decided the next day would find me back in hiding to study and photograph all I saw.

This time my vigil was as richly rewarded as my first encounter in the foothills had been empty. Here there was a magnificent house of immense proportions freshly daubed with mud. The pond behind the sturdy curving dam was alive with ducks that played over its mirrored surface. The marsh itself was riddled with canals, well-worn slides, and

piles of freshly cut willow and poplar limbs. But best of all there were beaver there—real live beaver, a pair of adults and four kits.

Winter was not far off. Dawn found a rind of frost covering the marsh weeds. The old pair had prepared well for it since great stocks of feed were piled beside the house. Now their main efforts were spent in making this structure a formidable fortress.

In the dim light I watched them swirl to the bottom of the pond, roiling up the water as they dug huge armfuls of mud, with which they emerged dripping and clutched to their breasts. Balancing on their broad tails and hind legs like animated tripods they staggered up the slippery side of the house to deposit their load.

91

In due course this was patted and smoothed like plaster, to eventually freeze solid, an impregnable structure even against the strong claws of any hungry predator who might later cross the ice of their frozen domain.

But strangely enough it was the kits that I found most intriguing. Their sense of fun was positively captivating. In common with most of the wild animals I have watched and photographed throughout the world, these four youngsters had each a delightfully distinct personality.

The one which attracted my attention most was the tiny chap who made a never-ending game of chasing one particular mallard duck that swam on the pond. At first I thought this was merely a passing thing. Perhaps just curiosity to see whether the duck would fly at his approach.

This did not happen. Instead the mallard would swim rapidly just out of his reach, the kit in hot pursuit, until just at the instant he was about to be touched he would start to tread water and flap out of reach while the beaver dived in sheer ecstasy of happiness.

Hour upon hour this went on. I wondered where the wee rascal got his energy and when the duck would find time to rest and feed. Obviously each revelled in the high spirit of fun, for instead of leaving the pond in desperation I saw the duck actually turn around and entice the beaver to further play by swimming towards him and quacking loudly when he showed signs of giving up the chase.

The second kit, it seemed, frowned on all this beaver play. For him life was a deadly serious business fully taken up with carrying small twigs no larger than a pencil to the woodpile, or patting down tiny particles of mud about the size of a dime on the monstrous dome of his home.

By sheer contrast the third one was as lazy as his brothers or sisters were energetic. Several times I nearly burst with fits of laughter as I watched him nonchalantly lying on his back and rolling over and over and over in the cool clear water. Nothing more to life than just that— rolling along!

Of the four, the last one seemed the least colourful in character. Though for expenditure of energy he fully equalled the first two. Feverishly he swam along the edge of the marsh, poking, probing, climbing over and under every clump of grass. He reminded me so much of modern man, eternally on the go searching for something, but not knowing what.

Occasionally I noticed that two of the kits would combine forces to try and corner a duck. In this they showed clever tactics and shrewd strategy. It was then that the mallards would take wing to the other end of the pond, only to return again in a few moments when the second kit had gone back to his rolling, mending, or searching, whichever the case might have been.

The entire day passed in this fascinating way, the placid scene accentuated by occasional visits from woodpeckers and 'whisky jacks', both of whom enjoyed digging in the fresh mud on the house. Only twice did the loud smack of an adult tail show displeasure at my presence, that, when because of my cramped position at the water's edge I moved too hastily and disturbed the tranquil setting.

93

By the time darkness closed in, the swiftly moving bodies of the kits could be discerned only by the tiny wake left in the water behind them.

It was time, too, for me to think of an evening fire and my meagre supper of soup and rice, but it would be enriched by memories of an hilarious day.

Another winter day I had a unique chance to watch a family of beaver whose pond was spring fed with warm water that prevented the ice from freezing over it solid. To my astonishment the adults would climb out on to the ice in broad daylight and make short forays through the deep snow in search of poplar limbs and willow twigs.

As an experiment I gathered some branches for them. One or two of these I pushed into the mud at the bottom with all my strength to see if any attempt would be made to pry them loose. It amazed me to see just how powerful a pull the old male could exert using his broad tail and webbed hind feet for bracing. With apparently little effort the limbs were quickly wrenched from the bottom and dragged away under water. A feat I would otherwise have thought impossible.

Beaver are actually not the crafty tree 'fallers' that they are often reputed to be. I have seen far too many of their cut trees that had lodged against others and never reached the ground. In fact, they do a tremendous lot of chiselling that yields few results for all their labour.

11
About Bears

So much has been written about bears that I almost hesitate to put pen to paper on the subject. Last winter I read an entire book which, from cover to cover, consisted of nothing else, so that by the time I was through I almost felt a little bearish myself.

In spite of all this it would not seem right, in a book of this sort, not to make at least some brief reference to these interesting creatures who add so much to the life of anyone who frequents wilderness country.

At the outset it is well to remember that some fantastic tales are told of bears, especially grizzlies, not all of which can be accepted as factual. A friend told me this one just after I returned from Africa.

A famous bow and arrow hunter who boasted of his daring feats in killing African big game came to British Columbia to kill a grizzly.

With a group of friends, who had scoffed at his exploits, he obtained the services of a guide. They were taken to a high mountain cabin in a small alpine glade where grizzlies were notorious. That evening they drew lots for first chance at a shot when the bear was spotted. Fortune smiled on the archer and he retired with this happy thought on his mind.

Sure enough at dawn there was a superb old 'silver tip' meandering about in view of the cabin. The elated archer sallied forth to do his daring deed while the others watched from the cabin, snickering to themselves.

When the crouched hunter approached him, the massive bear reared up on his hind legs in typical grizzly fashion to get a better view of the man. This unexpected action and the overwhelming height of the brute completely unnerved the archer. He turned to flee for the open cabin door. The curious grizzly, his interest aroused, gave chase in spirited fashion.

The bear had virtually overtaken the man and was literally breathing down his neck as they reached the cabin. An upturned root tripped the hunter who fell flat on his face before the open door. The grizzly, unable to check the speed of his own momentum, hurtled over the prostrate form and plunged through the doorway.

With acute presence of mind the brave archer leaped to his feet, hurriedly pulled the door shut behind the bear, then rushed around to the window and shouted to his detractors:

'When you get that one skinned, boys, I'll go get another!'

★   ★   ★

All encounters with bears are, of course, not quite this exciting, but it cannot be denied that they add a great deal of fun and colour to outdoor life. Even those which have become partially tame in the National Parks provide people with amusement and on occasion a rather unusual kind of semi-savage thrill.

One late October I was in the Yellowstone National Park. It was a glorious warm fall season without any cold incentive that would normally drive the bears to seek shelter for their winter's sleep. The tourist season was long past. The park was quiet and drained of traffic. Yet the bears persisted in lining the roads, hoping against hope that some miracle would happen and the lines of cars would reappear from which they could beg their bread.

Because this did not happen, and because they seemed to have forgotten the ancient instinct to search for bees, bugs, and berries to fatten them against the north winds, they were hungry and in a belligerent mood.

More out of pity than anything else I stopped to share my lunch with one unusually sad-looking old girl!. She obviously enjoyed the treat but was not ladylike enough to know when she had had her share. Instead of being grateful for small mercies she decided to try and take the bear's share by brute force.

With this in mind she plunged one big black arm through the car window to help herself. I attempted to talk her out of this hasty action, but obviously, as with most bears, words alone carried little weight. I started to run up the window so that it closed on her thick arm. It made little impression through the padding of dense hair and muscle. Instead she kept growling ominously and feeling around for more lunch which simply wasn't there.

Not wishing to become involved in an open conflict with my beneficiary, especially in a National Park, I felt a discreet withdrawal would be best. How did one go about breaking off diplomatic relations, especially in a case of this kind where one party was determined to press her case?

I decided to let the car roll ahead gently down the incline, hoping that the unexpected movement would unnerve my visitor and persuade her to withdraw. To my astonishment the old bear side-stepped neatly down the road, while she continued to fish around with her arm inside the car.

Not until we had attained a speed of nearly fifteen miles an hour did the old girl withdraw her arm and decide to drop off to the side of the road. Looking in the mirror I saw her testing the air with a weaving nose for one last faint fragrance of a lunch which she had hoped would last much longer than it did.

97

To my mind this aspect of wild creatures becoming dependent upon man for their sustenance is a rather sad feature about parks. So often the final result ends in death to the animals, either through starvation because the natural instincts to search for their natural food is lost, or because they become a pest and have to be destroyed.

Bears are and can be, when watched unnoticed, a magnificent part of our wild country. To see one of the old fellows fishing his favourite pool for trout or salmon is an absorbing display of cunning craftiness. To come across the fresh diggings of a grizzly where gigantic rocks are torn from their sockets in the soil can be a fine sensation. To watch a 1,000-pound bear strip the small blueberries from bushes with nimble dexterity is a show one will never forget.

At home in his own domain the bear is an astonishingly nimble fellow. The bulk and size which leads us to think of them as clumsy creatures is misleading. They can move with a swift silence that is uncanny. In the deep shade of thick forest their colouring blends with the shadows making them difficult to detect, an advantage they always make use of either in hunting or eluding the hunter.

Perhaps, though, by far the most appealing part of bear behaviour centres around the cubs. In my childhood home there was a unique photograph of twin cubs clinging to their mother's back in dense timber with the appropriate title, 'Babes in the Woods'. Since then my sympathy for the sternly disciplined youngsters has always been very real.

One afternoon in June I was resting beside the trail with my pack when across a distant stream on a rock slide I detected a light brown body moving. At first I was sure it was a cougar, but it disappeared into a thicket of vine maples before I could get the glasses on it. Taking my camera I started to inch towards the fast-flowing water. Just as I reached the stream I saw a black cub on top of a high rock on the other bank. Manœuvring through the thick undergrowth of mountain alders and vine maples to try and get a photograph I saw the old bear suddenly leap to the top of the rock.

With one sweeping cuff she sent her cub flying through the air to land in a tangle of brush below. She turned and gave me one disdainful look of 'beware' then plunged into the thicket herself. For several moments all I could see was a stormy tossing of limbs and brush tops as she ploughed through the tangle. A few yards farther on she emerged on to the rock slide with two cubs in tow, one pitch black like herself, the other a light fawn-coloured rascal which I had mistaken originally for a cougar.

Grunting short angry grunts of kof-kof-kof she drove and cuffed the twins up the slope at a double quick march. Nor did she slacken the pace until they had reached the sanctuary of some tall trees up which the cubs scurried while she mounted guard at the base.

I was not altogether sorry that the stream was too deep and wide for me to wade. At least it was a legitimate excuse for not following her into trouble, which I might have otherwise been tempted to do.

The next time that I had an opportunity to photograph this same combination of a black bear with different coloured twins I was with

99

a friend. We had seen the bears in a river bottom and it was decided that I would go down to see if I could move them into the open while he photographed them from on top of the bank.

Instead of just one bear and her cubs, there turned out to be a total of eight bears all milling around me in the willow thickets. This went on to the accompaniment of much rumbling and grumbling in bear language. My companion was sure that a colourful career in the wilds had at last come to its climax because I did not show up for a while. Actually I was engrossed in a lively game of hide and seek trying to get at least one good picture of the dark phantoms that slipped from shadow to shadow about me. The only photograph that was worth keeping from that episode shows one scarred old bear posed on the river bank, blending beautifully with the darkness of the woods behind him.

One could go on and on about bears, but this is not the place to do it. The only afterthought which I would wish to add pertains to the terrible tales of the dangerous grizzly. Here is an animal that needs to be treated with respect. If not molested or pressed he is seldom more vengeful than other wild creatures. His kind have been hunted and harried ruthlessly by man. If ever a species should feel that they have a score to settle with the human race it is the grizzly. He loves his remote back country and only rarely thrives where human beings make their inroads.

If cornered, wounded, or provoked when young are on hand they can become a terrible opponent. If, on the other hand, they are left to live their lives unmolested there is little ground for classifying them as aggressive and ill-tempered beasts.

Men are often unfair to the grizzly. They shoot him over baits of dead horses. They harry him for being a stock killer when in most instances all he has done is to clean up the carrion of animals that died from other causes. They have trapped, poisoned, and hunted this old man of the mountains with little thought for the day when over much of North America his kind will no longer wander. Then the cry will go up: 'Why didn't someone do something about it?'—after it is too late.

A friend of mine with a string of pack horses rode around a bend one day to come face to face with a huge grizzly and her cub. He reigned his mare to a halt. The hair rose on the grizzly's shoulders. The horse trembled as he spoke softly and gently to both her and the bear, who by now stood to her full height ready to charge. He continued to talk softly. The bear dropped to all fours, picked up her cub, tucked him under one arm, and backed away slowly. Arriving at a safe distance she put the cub down and the pair rolled away down the valley.

This is the sort of thing that convinces me that most of us simply do not give wild animals the benefit of the doubt. When we do they almost always demonstrate an attitude of forbearance 'of live and let live', which we human beings would do well to emulate. In that way both their lives and our days in the wilderness would be ever so much brighter.

101

12
Monarchs of the Marsh

IF MY first encounter with moose did nothing else, at least it rekindled that old, latent fire of enthusiasm for big-game photography that had burned so brightly during my boyhood. Because of the many demands made on my time, during the intervening years, by studies, business, and ranching, opportunities for serious photography had been few indeed. This was not for want of desire or dreaming about the pursuit, but first things simply had to come first.

So this memorable afternoon of which I now write marked the end of that 'camera-less' chapter in my life. Much more important, though, was the fact that it was to set in motion an enthralling future that would be closely bound up with wildlife studies and photography.

In spite of the fact that a gap of several years in Masailand were to occur between this first moose hunt and subsequent photographic forays after North American big game, I look back upon this unforgettable day in the marshes of Montana as the proper prelude to my serious wildlife photography in North America.

It was a golden October morning in the high mountain country of western Montana. I had stopped over to spend a few days on the Red Rock Lakes Trumpeter Swan Wildlife Refuge with my close friend Winston Banko, who was then manager of the preserve. This was one of several pleasant interludes for me during my journey back to East Africa.

Winston was anxious for me to see the wildlife of the refuge, and that morning we scrambled over the hills that towered above the great marshes. From the top we sighted two bull moose through the binoculars. They were feeding in the willow bottoms that skirted the marsh edge. On the spur of the moment we decided it would be good sport to attempt stalking them in the afternoon for a few pictures with Winston's camera, a big, bulky, box-type instrument.

We swallowed a hasty lunch, then headed for the marshes lest the moose move from where we had first seen them.

The wind was in our favour as we crouched and crawled through the tangle of broken willow clumps that had suffered so much from winter feeding by the big animals.

Beaver were busy in the willow thickets, too. Their dams had raised the water table in some parts and the willow brush was being drowned out. This meant that the surviving clumps would be browsed even more heavily than before if the moose population remained stable or increased.

We, too, were suffering from the effects of the beaver dams. Wading through the water and mud made us aware of their efforts in a very pointed manner.

All of a sudden we spotted a great black form peering through the brush at us. One of the bulls had lurched to his feet at our approach.

Winston meanwhile had been doing heroic work manœuvring his bulky camera through the morass of weeds, willows, and water. It was just from watching him wrestle with this equipment that I decided then and there that my future camera would be a compact, versatile instrument.

Trying to get a reasonably clear view of the bull through the lacework of tangled willow wands was quite a feat. Luckily the bull paused just long enough to allow himself to be photographed. Then with a splash he was away, shaking the spray from his head and hide. Our attempt had been a short-lived one indeed. None the less Winston sent me a print of that shot when I was in Africa. For a first trial it is remarkably impressive because of the mood created by the foreground tangle of branches—much out of focus—through which the head and antlers of the bull are clearly outlined.

Somewhat disappointed, we gurgled and floundered our way back out of the marsh. But my spirits had been set alight in that watery wilderness by the old black bull. Photographing big game on foot had posed a tremendous challenge, and I was going to do something about it! The old 'Monarch of the Marsh' had put fresh bone and sinew into my dreams that would be realized only after I had seen many more of his kind. Later attempts to photograph other species often brought me more encouragement than did my first moose hunts.

In the north country of British Columbia, a region where in recent times the moose has expanded his territory in an incredible manner, almost every year finds new logged-off areas and burned-over country of the province being occupied by this fascinating species. Because the moose is essentially a true woodland animal I have invariably associated him with the forests of Canada, and I am always delighted to hear of him flourishing in parts where he was never known before.

On the other hand my earliest contacts with moose were anything but smashing successes as the following incidents will show.

One morning before dawn I climbed a ridge overlooking a moose marsh set in a circle of timber and waited for daylight. With the rising sun I spotted two cows across the water feeding—up to their bellies in the grass.

As I debated whether or not to circle the swamp they suddenly tossed their heads and splashed away at full speed. With the sun directly behind them the flying spray kicked up by their feet and flung from their bodies was like a crystal fountain that engulfed them.

It astounded me to see them travel along through the marsh without slackening speed for at least two miles. The cause of their fear, I could only guess, was either wolves or a grizzly that had menaced them from the shore. They made directly across the expanse of water to my side of the marsh.

Secreting myself behind some shaggy spruce trees I watched them approach with heaving sides and dilated nostrils. A strong wind bent the trees along the water's edge and rippled the waves where a flock of coots fed in the shallows.

I got a photograph, poorly backlighted, of this setting just as the wind carried my scent to them. They whirled and sped for an island in the marsh where a thicket of dark pines swallowed them in its shadows.

Just then a Cooper's hawk dived on the coots right in front of me and they, too, took frenzied flight with madly flapping wings and fluttering feet.

A moment later, where there had been such a rich display of wild-life, now only the reeds nodded in the breeze as if to mock me and say: 'These moose aren't quite that easy to photograph.'

My next encounter with the great dark beasts was in a giant burn, littered with the black stumps and charred logs that remained from a forest fire. By dint of patient stalking I succeeded in creeping through the tangle of wreckage until I was within reasonable camera range. It impressed me as a spectacular and unique setting with the ungainly moose framed by the shattered skeletons of a once proud forest.

Much to my chagrin, when that film was processed it was found to be faulty and the photographs were worthless.

All of this may impress the reader as being depressing ground-work for a wildlife photographer. It was. But, just as from the ashes of a forest fire there may eventually emerge new and vigorous growth, so from my first set-backs with moose there were to unfold richly rewarding days of wildlife studies. It is not surprising, then, that in my affections there lingers a spot of tender regard for those rugged rascals who thrust me so roughly but surely into this new and enthralling career of animal photography.

13
Flowers, Ferns, and Fungi

IT IS always with some measure of trepidation that I deal with wild flowers. This is because there hovers over one the temptation to go on and on, eventually ending up with a catalogue that is bound to bore anyone who is not familiar with the varieties described.

On the other hand wild flowers are such a captivating part of our countryside, especially the alpine meadows in summer, that at least a few deserve attention. Each of us have our own favourites. I have elected to write briefly about those that have won a warm niche in my affections.

Strange as it sounds no plant spells s-p-r-i-n-g for me quite as eloquently as our flowering wild currant of the west. The bright burst of rich pink blossoms that lighten the woodland where they grow seem to declare winter at an end with gusto. One of these shrubs grew in the centre of one of my favourite meadows and had attained a height of about twelve feet and of equal size in circumference. When it started to glow in the spring half the world had to sing with it.

In recent years this has become an increasingly favourite ornamental for home gardens. I had a neighbour who took hundreds of cuttings from the wild bushes in his cut-over country and was marketing them to landscape gardeners.

Our wild native dogwood is another that has rapidly invaded city gardens. This arresting tree has been selected as British Columbia's provincial flower. Because of the public demand for young trees it was necessary to pass legislation making it unlawful to uproot dogwood trees from the forest.

Especially in areas like the east coast of Vancouver Island the dogwood is a common tree, which gives a bright splash of creamy white colour to the sombre forest. Some individual trees in favoured locations attain great size and are spectacular exhibits in full bloom. Pink specimens are rare but of exquisite beauty.

In direct contrast with the proud elegant dogwood is my humble friend the skunk cabbage or yellow Arum, found in the low marshy spots of the forest. I venture to say that this is one of the best known of our wild plants. Not necessarily for its beauty but also the aroma from which its common name is derived.

In spite of this, when I see the turgid spikes of immaculate yellow thrusting themselves up out of the mud and ooze of the swamps like candles in the dark my heart stirs with the fever of returning sunshine. I know, then, that the bears will be out feeding on those same shoots and summer is not far off.

A flower that I am fond of, not only for its own fragile beauty but also its useful function in healing over the cut-over country, is our fireweed. This is one of those hardy pioneer plants that invade the great burns and logged-off areas almost before any other vegetation can establish itself.

The light thistledown-like seed of the fireweed is scattered miles and miles on the faintest breeze. It piles up in drifts against logs, stumps, and rocks. In a year or two a waving sea of pink, mauve, and green covers the ghastly burn. The decaying vegetation from these plants soon adds organic matter to the scorched earth and provides a seed bed in which forest trees can once again re-establish themselves.

As though this alone was not service enough, their generous yield of amber honey is a delicacy that can seldom be matched for exquisite flavour. Pure fireweed honey on fresh home-made brown bread is a dish that knows few peers.

Where the fireweed is essentially a forest flower the mimulus is partial to the open places where there is ample moisture to sustain it. There are several members of the family; my two favourites being the yellow mimulus that clings to cracks and crevices in the rocks along the sea edge and the red variety that favours the stream edges and damp hollows of alpine meadows.

To find a plant of this type with a range from sea level to snow line is quite unusual. Several of my choicest plants actually grew where the winter storms drenched their rocks with spray day after day. At the other extreme I have found them growing in profusion at the very toe of a glacier 8,000 feet above sea level. The flower is a clean-cut handsome dash of brilliant colour that would attract anyone's attention who passed them on the trail.

Of the high mountain flowers none has ever quite stirred my imagination as has our avalanche lily or snow lily. Here is a delicate little plant of rare audacity. Even before all the mantle of snow has melted off the bosom of the upland country these plants will push their way up through the cold soil and even thin crusts of snow on occasion.

Scarcely have the snowdrifts disappeared from the slopes, when the drifts of countless hordes of avalanche lilies take their place in gay profusion. The nodding, curtsying crowds of white flowers with yellow throats are a sight to behold. Especially if we remind ourselves that each bulb has taken seven long years of growth before it ever dared to thrust a flower towards the waiting sun.

Perhaps the most picturesquely named of our wild flowers is the Indian paintbrush. This is an old old favourite with me. One is liable

to stumble on it almost anywhere at any time. Its brilliant orange-red hue sometimes varies from a sombre mauve to pale yellow depending on the type of soil and location where it is found.

Its stiff erect growth and bristle-like head might lead one to think that it was lacking in sweetness. Quite the opposite, for the hours I have watched humming birds visit these blooms proves otherwise. While, quite by surprise, I have learned that the flower heads themselves are a delicacy much in favour with deer and marmots, who will gorge themselves on this dish.

It is the great splashes of Indian paintbrush, intermingled with acres and acres of blue lupins, that give that rare sensation of elysian flower fields to our high country.

Blue lupins are not a particular pet of mine. Yet, because of their sheer weight in numbers alone, they merit inclusion here. I have often wished that the common lupins had a bolder, franker blue to them—something more closely akin to a bright October sky. In spite of their somewhat modest appearance they do lend a gentle hint of soft loveliness to any mountain landscape.

One hilarious experience I had with blue lupins is worth repeating here. A friend accompanied me on his first photographic jaunt into the mountains. Not owning a camera of his own at the time he used mine. The fields of lupins were at their peak and I could understand in a way why he should be thrilled by them. However, after several hours my curiosity became thoroughly aroused when he seemed to devote most of his time, effort, and pictures to lupins and lupins alone. It was as though he was drunk with these flowers and had gone on an orgy of lupin pictures. I began to make discreet remarks, not wishing to offend his taste in flowers, when, to my utter amazement, he disclosed that he was colourblind and the blue lupins were the only flowers that really aroused his enthusiasm.

When the pictures came back I nearly rolled off my chair laughing as we sat through slide after slide after slide of blue lupins. We still roar over this episode.

A blue flower to which I am very partial are the blue camas, commonly found along the seashore and islands on the coast. They have a lively blue that cannot be described and which of all the wild flowers are the most difficult to capture accurately on colour film. When great banks of these come into bloom along the cliffs with beyond them the sea white-capped, and the mountains snow-capped for a foil, one has a glimpse into the heart of a wild wonderland.

An unpretentious cousin of the blue camas are the white-flowered death camas. The two grow together indiscriminately. For sheep men, however, the death camas are a treacherous foe. The flower, leaves, and stems all contain a deadly poison which, if eaten by sheep, lambs in particular, proves fatal. One spring I lost seventeen lambs in this manner before we discovered what the cause was, and resorted to pulling the offenders out one by one, down on hands and knees.

Another wild flower that we had to contend with on the land was the common wild rose. In spite of the tremendous amount of labour I have had in eradicating these bushes from the abandoned fields I took over, they own a warm spot in my heart.

The fragile rose with its delicate perfume lasts only a single day. What a brief time to bloom and spread its sweetness! Because of the prolific show of blooms they make a fine display. Most important though are the rose hips which are a rich source of vitamin C, comparable to citrus fruits, and which remain as favourite delicacies for birds, chipmunks, mice, and squirrels who feed on them all winter. This happens to be Alberta's provincial flower.

So one could go on and on, but an end must come sometime. Otherwise I shall have a catalogue that includes everything from the dainty lady's slipper to the common dandelion.

Some mention must be made of our ferns. They are such a prominent part of the forest that they are familiar to everyone.

The largest and most conspicuous is the common bracken fern. This is always found where there are mild damp conditions. If the soil is fertile and of great depth I have measured them to a height of ten feet. In places on the coast their rank growth intermingled with wild roses or sallal can equal the most luxuriant tropical tangle I ever saw in Africa.

It is often in these fern patches where the deer and bear will bed down safe from prying eyes and yet be comfortable on a deep mat of crushed stems and fronds.

On farmland the bracken is really a friend in disguise. If allowed to grow unchecked, the great mass of spreading roots will soon invade

 113

and completely take over a field. If cut repeatedly with a mower or ploughed under, the huge accumulations of decaying leaves and rotting roots contribute richly to the organic matter in the soil which they have already rendered open and friable with their root systems.

The sword fern is a true woodland species not found in the open as the bracken. They often form giant colonies in cool moist spots, deep in the shade cast by the overhanging canopy of cedars, fir, and spruce. The leaves are typical long sword-like structures sometimes attaining as much as four feet in length. Usually they are of a deep rich green colour that adds much to the attractiveness of the forest floor.

This is the fern commonly harvested by the Indians' and loggers' children for the florists. The fronds are packed in great shining bundles and shipped from their misty wet home on the coast to all points on the continent.

A much less conspicuous fern is the common little wood fern that is found almost everywhere in the Canadian woods. It grows on old logs, around rocks, on decaying vegetation of almost any kind and is a hardy companion almost anywhere one travels in the back country.

The maiden's hair is no doubt amongst the most fragile and beautiful of our native ferns. Any time I come to a rapids, a waterfall, a bit of white water along a stream edge I instinctively expect to find a spray or two of maiden's hair leaning over the spot. It is as though its main purpose in life was to keep its dainty head drenched with droplets of moisture that bounced from the foam and spray beneath it.

Finally we come to the fungi, lowly forms that rank high in my estimation of woodland fare. No fall would be complete for me without a good many feeds of delicious wild mushrooms. Just the adventure of going afield in search of fresh mushrooms is something like prospecting for gold. It has the advantage of more often turning out a complete success, too, if one knows where and what to look for.

The common white meadow mushroom with the pink gills is one that everyone knows. Where horses have pastured they will appear in profusion after the first fall rains. Then is the time to go afield with baskets and buckets, returning with them brimming full.

One variety quite similar to the meadow mushroom but less common and often found in the woods is the Destroying Angel. This tempting morsel contains one of the most potent plant poisons occurring in Nature. It has no pink gills and for that reason should never be plucked.

Another delectable morsel is the humble little puff ball. These should be taken just at their prime while the flesh is firm and white. Sliced thinly, fried in butter and garnished with garlic salt they are a gourmet's delight.

The Blue Bonnets are not only colourful and of interest when found in the meadows but if not too old almost as delicious as the meadow mushrooms. One fall I discovered several patches of this variety in a bracken field which provided many fine meals over a

115

period of several weeks. This is quite a favourite, too, with deer, who eat large quantities of mushrooms in the autumn.

A unique variety which many, not familiar with it, would consider poisonous is our Shaggy Mane. The grotesque bullet-shaped cap with flaking scales will thrust itself up through a crack in the hardest soil. The black gills and masses of black spores frighten anyone not already shy of it. Yet in reality it is a fine dish and one which I harvest every year. The choicest group of this mushroom that I ever found was protruding right through a crack in the centre of a new piece of pavement.

The dainty fairy ring mushroom that has led to so many fairy tales for children is also edible. The individuals are so tiny that, in most instances, people will not take the trouble to gather them. The only way in which they are seen by many city people is when the fairy rings show up in their prize lawns. Then they become a detestable thing to be destroyed. For me they are the places where fairies and goblins dance on the dew-drenched grass at night.

In direct contrast with the fragile fairy ring mushrooms is our giant Clitocybe. This is the most massive of our woodland mushrooms. Some individual specimens I have seen were as large as a dinner plate. When they burst up out of the forest floor with bits of leaves, bark, and needles adhering to them they are a spectacle of strength.

The flesh, though edible, is coarse and lacks the delicious flavour of other smaller mushrooms. In fact the flesh of the Clitocybe in Canada cannot be compared in any way with that of the giant mushrooms in Africa. These latter I have seen of such a size that even a dik-dik could shelter under them from the rain.

Perhaps the showiest of our mushrooms is the brilliant orange-capped fly Agaric. This is a poisonous species. Often one will find them eaten by insects which had dropped dead close by. They are readily distinguished by their gaudy colouring.

A last interesting fungus is the bracket fungus which grows on the bark of our forest trees. The colourful white upper surface is sometimes employed by artists as a place on which to paint attractive scenes of the countryside in which all these lower forms of plant life are such a fascinating part.

14
Magic in the Mountains

FOR as far back as I can remember mountains have held a mysterious fascination for me. Perhaps this can be attributed to the fact that my ancestors were Swiss, for whom the Alps composed both the outer circumference and inner core of life.

One of my fondest childhood memories is that of sitting at the upper bedroom window of our bungalow in Africa and watching the equatorial sun rise in red glory behind the ragged ramparts of the Nandi Hills. Nor was I content to merely dream about those bold bluffs of rock and forest that pushed against the eastern skyline. By the time I was in high school I had hunted and explored most of their shaggy crest.

At fifteen I tackled Mount Kilimanjaro and became violently ill in the assault. The bitterest cup to drink came, when, after making camp at 15,000 feet, I awoke the next morning to find myself surrounded with an unusual fall of deep fresh snow that forced me back down to the Masai Plains.

I have recounted earlier the strong pull of the mountains that drew me to the north-west section of North America, and of the glorious summer spent up on old Mount Rainier.

Naturally there were, on occasion, wide gaps of time between those various episodes in the high country. Yet there persisted that deep passion to seek the high places whenever the chance came along.

At Fair-Winds I would gaze across the straits of Juan de Fuca at the tantalizing loveliness of the Olympics and yearn for their snow-fields, spires, and alpine meadows. Meanwhile my feet were tethered to a ranch.

Not until I returned from Africa a second time, with my health to mend, and a little leisure in which to do it, did I really become intimately acquainted with that remarkable range. What I found in the back wilderness of the Olympics was a new love that has grown in intensity with each succeeding summer. I have explored a goodly number of different ranges now and each new expedition holds magic in the making.

Basically there is a variety of reasons why I go frequently to the mountains. Very briefly they may be catalogued under the following headings: (a) For invigoration of body. (b) For rejuvenation of spirit. (c) For a proper perspective of mind. (d) For the deep contentment of living simply amid unspoiled wilderness grandeur. (e) For the exhilaration of meeting a challenge and taking chances. (f) For opportunities to live with, study, and photograph wildlife.

Though much of the emphasis in this book is upon the last phase, that does not mean that it is necessarily the most important. Stalking and photographing game are bound to hold some interest even for the casual reader who may have little desire to go climbing himself. On the other hand, for those who find themselves hankering for the heights I have written this chapter in order to share with them a little of my mountain enthusiasm.

Climbing and hiking in high country with perhaps a thirty-pound pack on one's back can be, if one is not accustomed to it, a grim game. Shortness of wind, aching legs, sore shoulders, general lassitude, and depression are all indications that the body is not fit nor trimmed to the task.

Surprisingly enough, with a little practice and perseverance, the human frame can adjust itself to these new demands in a remarkably short time. By this I do not think in terms of hours but rather days, or if one is hopelessly out of shape, perhaps even weeks.

On at least four occasions I have had un-hardened companions who met their defeat on the slopes simply because they had made no physical preparation to toughen themselves for the ordeal. There are few sights indeed quite as pathetic as that of a full-bodied man 'out' on his back, gazing longingly at the summit, but beaten with no choice but to retreat down the slope.

In contrast, the challenge of the peaks, when met in the full vigour of rawhide muscles, can be a dynamic experience. Sound wind and strong legs seem willing to achieve more than one might otherwise feel they could attain when under the stimulus of a mountain's magic.

Then it is one comes down off the ridges with trimmed weight, elastic muscles, deep chest, clear brain, and bright eyes. This is to feel fully alive, charged with vibrant energy.

What the high country can do for the body, it can also accomplish for the human spirit. The rather regrettable thing is that only a handful of people are aware of this alchemy. Like most things pertaining to man's spirit it is something which has to be tried, tasted, and tested to convince us that it is really so.

There is afoot a very influential school of thought which maintains that mountain wilderness country should be made more readily accessible to the masses. It is their contention that more highways, more charter aircraft, more railroads into modernized tourist centres are the answer to the frustrations of our jaded suburbanites. Actually this is not so. I have stood askance watching tourists more engrossed in their dime novels and week-end comics than the breath-taking panorama surrounding them on a mountain look-out. This, in spite of the fact

that they may have driven 3,000 miles and climbed 6,000 feet in their high-powered cars to view this spectacle.

No, the nub of the question is something too subtle to be solved by merely driving more roads into remote wilderness. It is the humble art of learning to attune our souls to the harmony of the wilds around us when we go afield.

Not everyone during life's brief sojourn is going to have a chance to climb the Rockies, Alps, or Himalayas—nor must they, to enjoy the rejuvenation of spirit which the wilderness can provide. A hill at home, a seaside cliff, or any handy height of land can provide the same sensations if tackled on foot with an open receptive heart.

A portion of the balm that is laid upon the frayed nerves and dull spirit lies in the simple bodily effort of getting to the top. Somehow, this time, these precious hours or days carved from the dull round of daily living and devoted to a different aim, becomes enshrined in our memories.

Instead of half listening to some radio blaring its baneful bedlam, we suddenly find ourselves tuning our ears to the sound of a skylark suspended in song against the blue of heaven. Instead of shuffling along cement sidewalks on aching arches, we discover again the spring and bounce of turf under our toes and soft spruce needles on our path. Nostrils seared and staled with exhaust fumes and factory smoke suddenly twitch and thrill to the teasing fragrance of wild blossoms and pinewood resins. Lips that have tasted only chlorinated tap water tingle at the caress of a clear mountain brook. Eyes fogged with TV, tawdry advertisements, and traffic lights brighten with the broad sweep of mountain valleys and tumbled hills.

Slowly there seeps into the spirit an awareness that these things are, after all, part of the rich living earth to which man belongs. They are not bits and pieces, unrelated playthings that belong to him merely for amusement. They, with him, are part of a dynamic entity, a simple whole, which if he recognizes his proper part in the scheme of things will give a balanced purpose to his life. His very being will have reason to it as he draws fresh strength for his spirit from his surroundings. Thus rejuvenated he can return to face anew the grinding mill of man-made city life. There the sublime integrity of the human individual ordained from the beginning of time is so readily lost under the massive pressures of a conforming society. There men and women so often despair of life. There they lose touch with reality. There life lacks direction and drive.

But for those who have tasted it, there remains a looking forward, a deep yearning for the next trip into high country where the mountains can work their magic.

The third reason I gave for going to the mountains was for a proper perspective of mind. Unless the reader has been privileged to find himself in real mountain country, this will be a difficult idea to grasp.

Somehow there is about true mountains a might, grandeur, and loftiness not to be felt anywhere else on the earth. Nor can these impressions be etched on the mind except through the effort of climbing them on foot.

During the slow ascent there is ample time to reflect on one's own insignificance in the face of such tremendous massifs.

Often the trail will lead initially through mile upon mile of magnificent virgin forest. It is a sobering thought to stop and reflect upon the startling fact that not a single one from these multitudes of tall trees had ever been planted, tended, or nourished by a man's hand. This was God's work!

It is humbling, too, to break from the cool dim shadows of timberline into the brilliant pageantry of 10,000 acres of alpine flower-fields—a sight so utterly celestial that even the most pretentious man-made gardens appear as ragged imitations on a rag doll's scale.

Man has made so much of his engineering feats upon the face of the earth; his mighty dams; his piles of brick and concrete; his millions of cubic yards of earth and rock moved with machinery. When viewed beside the colossal accumulation of material in a single mountain like Mount Robson it makes us wonder that we have the audacity to brag at all.

Then, as I sit in silent meditation by my camp-fire and from the heights perchance see the distant twinkle of lights, I begin to compare things. There, below me, are the flash of cars, trains, neon signs, and human industry. How tiny they are, yet they loom so large in the lives of those who must live always near the 'bright lights'. Perhaps that is why so many of us are blind to other shimmering lights that twinkle

overhead: lights of stars, planets, suns, and galaxies so immense, our finite minds cannot comprehend them. I gaze in wonder at the universe and marvel at my own insignificance.

With such a feeling upon one it is not too difficult to allow material things, the 'front' of social life, and the bias of human thinking, to fall into proper perspective.

This then prepares one for that delightfully satisfying experience of living quietly, humbly, and unobtrusively amid such glories. This being my next main reason for going to the mountains.

Gone is the prestige of living on the élite side of the tracks. Far removed is the standard of social deportment demanded by the rank or office of the life left behind. Here, as in the arctic, the desert, or the jungle a man's a man for all of that.

A drink from a glacier stream equals wine from the thinnest glass. Soup and rice spiced with conifer needles needs no caviar to whet the appetite. Weary muscles sink to rest on spruce boughs without the soporific stimulus of sleeping pills or spring-filled mattresses. The challenging bugle of a bull elk ringing across the frosty night air is the music of a master.

Simple things—yes. Simple life—yes. But how intrinsically rich.

Stripped of its veneer and artificial ornamentation, human life can take on genuine dignity amid such surroundings. Callous, indeed, must be the soul of anyone not moved to more noble thought and purpose by such surroundings. Here one comes face to face with primal beauty which, if a mortal will but allow it, can reflect something of its own winsomeness in his personality. Few are those I have known who lived much among the mountains that were not better men and women for the sincerity that was in their souls.

No doubt it is my intense individuality, my rebellion against the ever-growing pressures made on human beings to compress them into a single mould that takes me to the mountains for their challenge and their risks.

The world around, men and women are growing up in societies which lay ever-increasing emphasis upon security. Almost from the cradle to the grave various nations have devised methods to ensure that the individual will be secure in education, in health, in employment, in welfare of old age. Since all these services come at a price, not only

in terms of money, but also personal freedoms, the old slogan of 'safety first' is rapidly acquiring a world-wide application. The net result is that individuals are losing the old spirit of adventure; the willingness to take a chance; the desire to meet a challenge.

The mountains are a natural amphitheatre for the adventuresome to find an outlet for their deep wild cravings. It was the late Sir Henry Segrave (speedboat driver) who made the remark that: 'No man has truly lived any day in which he did not feel he had risked his life.'

There is much truth in it. In some mysterious way responding to the call of the unscaled peak; tackling this knife ridge; working across the face of that dangerous slope imbue one with an alertness of mind and muscle tuned to their highest pitch that is otherwise impossible.

By this I do not refer to ridiculous stunts or foolhardy showmanship that imperils life and limb. What I am speaking of is the coolly calculated risk, the calm acceptance of a challenge, that when successfully attained leaves that inner glow of self-respect and strength. Then comes that power of knowledge and trust in one's own inner resources and self-reliance.

Finally, of course, is that tremendously, for me, exhilarating aspect of the mountains—wildlife. Without it my experiences would be something like potatoes without gravy. Solid enough, but the topping makes the difference.

Wildlife place an aura of fascination about mountains which trees, flowers, ice, snow, and storms can never do. It lies in the fact, I think, that here are fellow creatures—living flesh, blood, and bone—who have identified themselves with this glorious high country. By living quietly with them—following, stalking, studying, learning, and photographing—a whole new magical realm of gripping drama reveals itself.

15
Woodland Harvest

THE common concept of forest management and timber crops is in terms of logs, lumber, pulpwood, paper, firewood, shingles, piling, and plywood. This chapter is not about these products, important as they may be in the economy and life of this country. Whole books may be obtained on any single one of the above subjects. Nor, on the other hand, are they by-passed here because I have no first-hand knowledge of them; quite the reverse. For to tell of the forest camps and sawmills I have worked in, the logs I have choked, yarded, and dumped into

the 'salt chuck', or the toil and sweat of cutting, peeling, and hauling pulpwood would in itself be a lengthy and, I fear, somewhat dismal tale. In any event it has been told so often before in a dozen different ways by men who have spent their entire lives at the game that it requires no repetition here.

Rather my intention is to try and share with the reader some of those mellow moods and moments that can be had for the taking. Pleasures which anyone who cares to go afield in the forest and cut-over country searching for less spectacular crops can enjoy.

There will not be that aura of mechanical might which surrounds the whine of chain saws, the crash of timber, the snorting cats, and screeching cables of a logging show. Lacking from the peaceful pursuits I describe will be the powerful pulse of mammoth trucks and piles of logs on the move to the mill.

Instead come with me away to the dimly lit trails trodden by the moccasined feet of an Indian boy in search of fern fronds. Or perhaps with his sister he will be plucking the greenery of sallal and huckleberry.

Coming from the damp softness of the Pacific slope with its gentle winter rains the glistening green foliage will be bundled, wrapped, and shipped to the rest of a shivering nation frozen deep under a six months' long blanket of winter.

Perhaps those sword ferns and sallal will form a wreath to lie at the foot of a snow-mantled cenotaph 3,000 miles away in Montreal or Halifax.

When fall arrives and the first winter storms send the squirrels scampering to the tree-tops to cut their winter supply of cones, the cone harvest will commence for humans, too. The seeds, tightly packed in the cones, are ripe and ready to collect.

Thousands upon thousands of sacks of seed are gathered—some of which ultimately find their way around the world to forest-producing lands.

Those who make a serious business of cone gathering will follow the fallers and collect their crop from the prostrate trees. Others more daring will climb prolific trees to fill their sacks. But most are content to casually follow in the little squirrel's footsteps, allowing him to set the pace at which the trees are cropped.

Above and beyond all of these, however, is a crop of exquisite delicacy and flavour—wild berries. Of these there are a goodly number from which to choose, but the best known by far are the wild blueberries and wild blackberries. Others less popular are salmon berries, thimble berries, black caps, and brambles with many borderline varieties esteemed by the birds but shunned by man.

Generally, though not always, the finest blueberries are found on cut-over land. Although I have had some sumptuous feeds from blueberry patches growing in the heart of the forest. Again as one emerges from the timbered slopes into the alpine country this fruit becomes prolific and is a popular part of the diet for birds and bears. The tangy taste of blueberry pie established a reputation for this dish almost from the first summer that white men set foot upon the continent.

Unlike the blueberry and its cousin the huckleberry which are found from coast to coast, our north-western blackberry is a species peculiar to the northern Pacific coast. This little berry with its thin, thorny vines which cling and cover old stumps, windfalls, and down timber possesses a delicate flavour unmatched by any other fruit of this type.

The berries themselves are, when compared with loganberries, himalayas, boysenberries, or other cultivated types, of most insignificant size. Yet I dare to say that there only do they suffer by comparison. For a dish to stir the imagination and garnish the palate they have no peer. Served as a shortcake smothered under thick whipped cream they are a foretaste of the very fruits of paradise itself.

The gathering of these berries is a fascinating challenge. They are somewhat temperamental in their yield from year to year, depending, of course, on the kind of summer weather. Dry, hot summers result in dried shrunken fruit, difficult to pick, and lacking sweetness. Excessive rains yield large berries, but frequently poor in flavour.

Competition for the dainty morsels comes from crows, coons, robins, bears, and other ardent human pickers who have learned where the best patches are generally found.

To pack a picnic lunch and head up some unfamiliar logging road in search of wild blackberries is to set sail on a day of high adventure. By dark your body may well be bruised from scrambling and tumbling through a dozen windfalls; your hands and lips will be purple with the stain of the lovely juice and your skin will be punctured, torn, and scratched by the hooked thorns. Perhaps clothing will be awry and damaged beyond repair—but if your bucket is brimming with the precious fruit you will feel like calling the whole wide world to share in your triumph.

16
Outdoorsmen

ON THE tangled trails of my relentless wanderings in wild country I have encountered an assortment of men and women from every walk of life; people from diverse backgrounds; with every sort of character and personality. Happily amongst many of them there could be found a trait which above all others bound us together with a common tie of comradeship—and that was a love for the wilds.

This powerful force at work in a person's life can somehow surmount barriers between human beings which otherwise could alienate strangers for ever. Take a professor, a street sweeper, a clergyman, and a rancher—none of whom have anything of a social character to attract them to each other—but let them be bird watchers, mountain climbers, or butterfly collectors and a basis for firm friendships is established at once.

Added to this is the hauntingly mysterious yet delightful fact that more often than not the calm solitude of wilderness surroundings tends to bring out the best in folk. It is beside a mellow camp-fire or under the awesome grandeur of a mountain peak that one man will commune with another about those deep inner feelings that are buried in his heart: feelings which normally are suppressed by the false front and hard crust that is built up to survive in the scramble of our selfish society.

Inevitably any progress which may be made in our attitude to the unspoiled countryside must start with individuals. The care with which a father puts out his camp-fire before moving on will prove a more profound lesson for his youngsters than any lecture in school on the subject. In the same manner if he will play the game and show a high calibre of sportsmanship in hunting, fishing, or camping, the net result will be to produce children with a right regard for natural resources that no amount of legislation or law enforcement officers could ever instil in them.

There are instances where young people may not be blessed with parents who enjoy the out-of-doors. Or the circumstances of life may make it impossible for the family to be out together. At such times children who have a natural affinity for the wilds either have to learn things for themselves the hard way or rely on strangers to take a kindly interest and introduce them to this new world.

I have been most fortunate in enjoying not only the comradeship of my parents who were so much in harmony with the wilds, but also the companionship of many strangers along the new trails I chose to follow after leaving home. Because these men and women do play such an important though unsung part in preserving the wild country I have decided to include thumbnail sketches of several in this book.

This I do out of a sense of deep gratitude for both the wisdom of the wilds they imparted to me and also for their own intrinsic worth as individuals and friends. In order that they should not be embarrassed

I have chosen to use names other than their own. If perchance any of them should read these pages they would no doubt recognize themselves at once. If so, it is my genuine hope that they will feel honoured by the description.

★   ★   ★

DUSKY

His home had always been the tangle of little lakes, bays, islands, waterways, and rough broken country of northern Ontario. I doubt if by the age of thirty he had travelled in any one direction more than a hundred miles from the rough log cabin in which he was born. Yet the terrain that lay within that circle of a 100-mile radius was to his moccasined feet as familiar as the floor of his canoe.

He knew where every family of beaver had built their houses and backed up their ponds behind brush dams during his last twenty years of life. What was more, he understood exactly how many could be trapped each winter without reducing their numbers to a dangerous level.

It was he who taught me where the small-mouthed bass lurked in the lakes. He unfolded for me the lore of the north, the rhythm of its seasons, the charm that lay beneath its harsh exterior.

When first I came to his country of barren rocks, poplar trees, and stunted conifers I could see only the greyness of the granite and the naked wind-tossed limbs. He taught me to find the warmth of pine-knot fires and roasted fish.

My early summer was an agony of enduring vicious mosquitoes and hungry black flies. He helped me to understand that without them the lakes and rivers would not be stirred with the silver flash of feeding fish or swallows sweeping low across the glinting surfaces.

Together we slipped unnoticed through the back waters in his canoe. Silent as a wind-blown leaf he drove it across the surface with sharp deft strokes. Along our route he introduced me to the mysteries of his woodland friends. Here the red squirrel in her nest, there a ruffed grouse on his drumming log; beyond the pond a teal with her brood hiding in the marsh grass.

133

Fall came in a glory known only to the North. Softly we walked the deer trails. Softly he told me of the wolf call in the night. Like a shadow he moved silently through the shadows. It was as though he was one of them. He was, for he was an Indian.

OLD SALT

The very first time we met I took to him instinctively. Eyes of deep sea blue danced in the brown wind-burned face that had stood the lashing of Pacific storms. When he talked it was with the gentle sound of a slack tide that whispered over a sand spit, soft and musical.

How he loved the rugged grandeur of the gale-chiselled coastline! He loved it so deeply it had virtually chiselled itself into the rugged character that lined his own face, and muscled his body.

We were destined to sail often together. Sometimes it would be into the teeth of a westerly that threw us back on our stern and made the ship's timbers quiver in the struggle to right herself. The wind whipped past us to hurl its spray and salt into the stunted timber that clung to the cliffs above the black rocks. He would give me a wink, grin a bit and remark: 'She's sure twisting our tail today!'

Anchored in a quiet bay we would take the skiff and skirt the shore. Here we explored for clams and crabs; we followed the footprints of a coon and watched the flights of brant that were heading for Alaska.

He taught me to love the big timber of the west coast. He showed me the wonders of the deep shadows where salmon berries, thimble berries, and a host of other strange wild fruits flourished.

In the tiny galley of his ship we prepared feeds of crab, oysters, clams, and fish that could only come from the hands of one with salt water in his veins. Perhaps their delicacy could be attributed in part to our moonlight forays ashore to gather the delectable morsels for our feeds.

He took special delight in cruising casually amongst rock reefs, islands, and promontories where the sea-birds built their nests and the seals came to bask in the summer sun.

Every summer he loaded up youngsters from scattered settlements along the lonely coast that was his happy hunting ground and took

them to a camp. There they had a fresh look at the great wide world in which they lived, and with the look came a chance to know the One who had originally designed and set it all in motion.

Few men on this coast are loved as he is loved. To him there is no front, no sham, no pride. Whether in a humble seaside cottage or in a mansion on the main drive his simple shining spirit warms the home and cheers the heart. For me it is a high honour to count him as one of my closest friends.

THE DOCTOR

Every Sunday morning that it was possible I listened to him speak over the radio, and this went on for ten years before I ever met the man. We had corresponded, we had developed a bond of understanding, but we had never met.

He was a preacher, and as preachers went with me a most unique type, for his messages dealt with such unlikely subjects as 'Timberline', 'Canyons', 'High Tide', and 'The Avalanche Lily'.

What gripped me was that he made the simple things of the wide open places take on a meaning that has stirred my heart again and again. That must be something like the feeling the crowds had who followed Christ around the countryside listening to his homely earthy chats about sheep, wheat, flowers, birds, and foxes.

The remarkable thing is that even now after many years I can still recall entire talks that this man gave. This for me is incredible since I honestly confess that in most church services I sit there dreaming about mountains, plains, wild goats, bears, lions, or elephants while the minister struggles with such profundities as the millennium, the transfiguration, or indoctrination.

For me the simple fact that I found a man who could tie together the wonders of God's earth with the wonders God wants to perform in my own heart was a remarkable discovery. In fact few men have enriched my entire life more, and certainly none have ever enabled me to see more clearly the simple and basic reasons for my very existence, and the purposes for which I happen to have been placed on the planet.

Finally, after long years of waiting, the Doctor came to visit in my home. Together we took a walk along the rugged shore on a wintry February day. He paused at one of the little shale beaches and raised a finger. A gentle breeze sighed in the spruce trees and lifted the waves that lapped on the beach.

'Hear those two sounds?' He smiled as he said it. 'That's some of the first music that man ever listened to.'

Little wonder his pulpit is regarded amongst the ten greatest in North America today!

FIRE RANGER

He was long, lank, raw boned like a colt, with a booming voice and infectious laugh that shook his loose hinged frame to the toes of his hefty hiking boots.

He and I had laughed together in the mountain cabin until my ribs ached from the strain. Yes, solid wholesome laughter spiced with the clean cool air that slides down off mountain glaciers.

Our backgrounds were a world apart. He came from an American city home; I came from the African bush. But we both loved the wilderness.

Across the years our paths have been far apart but our hearts are still one. From time to time we manage to be together just long enough to make a short mountain trip and rekindle the old enthusiasm.

As a trained scientist in his own field he has enjoyed appointments across the country that enabled him to delve into the life habits of the wild creatures under his care.

Sad to say, as is the lot of so many of the 'better' outdoorsmen in government service, they find there lies a fork in the upward path. If they are to advance it is generally into the confinement of an office desk and paper duties. To choose the other path is to sacrifice promotion, pay, and other benefits which at times the wilds may still make up to a man, but may not to his family. Happily my friend has been entrusted with the weighty load of managing much of the habitat on the wildlife refuges of the United States.

It is a comforting thought that at least a few of his calibre are in places of authority. With his kind at the helm, we won't get far off course in preserving our wildlife. More power to the old rascal!

17
A Northern Lake

IT HAS never been my lot in life to live on the shore of a lake. I have hunted, fished, canoed, camped, and swum in lakes all over the earth; but to have actually lived beside one long enough that it came to be a part of me is a sensation I have yet to enjoy. I am told that lakes, that is, small lakes, have a soft tranquillizing influence on personality. This is in direct contrast to the surging stimulus of seas, especially the storm-lashed spectacle of grey winter water that hurls itself in foam and fury on the headlands around my home.

Sometimes, purely for inspiration, I go to stand on a black rock bluff back of the house and there watch the glory of a gale. The resonant reverberation of tons of grey-green water booming against granite is music that was set in motion when the first wave made impact with virgin, upthrust land at the dawn of time. Nor has the melody ceased to encircle our planet since that epic hour, rising and diminishing in volume only with the changing key of the seasons.

This rhythm of tidal waters is lacking from lakes, even the largest lakes. My boyhood home in Africa was perched high on a cool escarpment eight miles from the shores of Lake Victoria, the world's second largest freshwater lake. Occasionally we would go down to the shore to picnic under the gigantic spreading limbs of wild fig trees that grew by the shore. I knew that there could be violent storms and squalls on that placid sheet of water. Islands of papyrus and marsh grass that had been torn loose from their anchorage in the shallows by the wave action would drift across the lake and be driven on to the shore by the wind. Yet I never witnessed a storm myself.

Actually the water was generally so placid that its greatest attraction was as a surface on which to skip stones. Swimming we could do only at the risk of providing the crocodiles with fresh meat. Bird life was abundant, and occasionally I had the thrill of watching hippos bask in the water, the old cows with their babes on their backs. The only time the old lake ever really roused me was one moonlight night when my father and I drove down to the shore especially to see if we could find hippos out grazing. Our luck held and there, sure enough, looking as big as box-cars under the moonglow, were several of the old bulls mowing down the grass in armfuls. No animals ever loomed quite so large before my eyes as did those hefty lords of the lake.

So it was not until I had visited many more lakes, especially those in Canada, that they began to comprise an important part of my life. To describe or even tell a few of the adventures that are entwined around 'my' lakes would be to weary the reader. Instead of which I have decided to recount the events of one twenty-four-hour period which no doubt is the only brief contact I shall probably ever have with this particular gem.

My quest was for moose. The time of year was late spring, just before calving. The object was to photograph them just as they moved from the lower levels of the winter range, following the receding snow-line up to fresh summer grounds. I had been told of a tiny, mountain-ringed lake in northern British Columbia where conditions should be ideal for the purpose because of the restricted area in which the moose moved.

With a heavy pack and a light heart I started into the woodland trail, expecting that I would be gone about ten days. Obviously I was the first human being over the trail that year. The blow-downs and tangle of winter wreckage across my path made travel a series of scrambles up and down over the windfalls.

139

Long ago the black mud of the trail in the willow bottoms had been ploughed deeply with the hooves of the wintering herd. Now spring rain had softened the furrows and filled the depressions. Few fresh tracks were to be found and I wondered if I was too late. Sunshine streamed into the valley, filling it with a warm haze that hung in the trees and warmed the rock slides. The snow had melted earlier than usual under the embracing warmth of spring and now gorged every gully and stream-bed with gushing freshets.

If moose tracks were scarce, bear prints were not. The great oval paws of a grizzly reminded me to keep a watch for the owner on the rock slides above the lake shore where he would be hunting for marmots and mice.

By the time I had reached the lake edge my feet were wet from wading so many watercourses, which a week earlier would have been dry. The level of the lake was at its maximum, lapping the lower branches and fresh lush leaves of the trees and foliage that girdled it.

But it was beautiful!

It was gleaming with the washing of spring rains and polishing of spring sunlight. Gone was the greyness of rotten ice and melting snow, the debris of wind-littered winter twigs. Its surface of blue that bounced and sparkled with a million points of reflected light was broken by a beckoning island of rock and birch trees.

The hard haul to get there had already been paid for by the beauty before me, even if I did not see another thing.

The forest fringe was garbed in an array of greens that I hardly knew existed. This Cariboo country of British Columbia is rich with a profusion of trees and shrubs. Conifers and deciduous trees were intermingled in magnificent disarray. Their bold brown barks or glistening sheaths of white formed a foil that reflected clearly the surface of the lake.

I decided to circle the shoreline in search of moose sign. There was none; only the cast-off antlers of last year and the old brown, almond-shaped pellets compressed from digested willow twigs. Suddenly I chanced on a boat that had been cached the previous summer. This would be much better than wading the shore.

As noiselessly as possible I dipped the oars and drifted off with the wind. My pack no longer dragged at my shoulders. I luxuriated in the release. I let the breeze blow through my hair and the sun play on my chest.

It took me quite a time to find the main stream that fed the lake. It proved to be a limpid lovely thing that wound its way around the giant buttresses of spruce, cedar, and hemlock of the valley floor. Its banks were padded with two trampled trails where the bears had been haunting the pools for spawning trout.

Shafts of sunshine pierced the dense canopy of limbs overhanging the stream and found their mark in the water. There I watched the fish hovering over their reds in the gravel, perpetuating the species in spite of floods, bears, and other natural hazards. It took a little careful manœuvring before I finally photographed the trout successfully. They kept mistaking me for a hungry bear and would dart off into the shadows for protection. I could hardly blame them for obviously the well-worn bear tracks at the water's edge were mute evidence of their persecution.

Back on the lake again I drifted silently along its verge, scanning the rock slides for grizzlies. Marmots, the yellow-bellied kind, whistled from their boulder look-outs, but it must have been me that disturbed them, for I saw no grizzlies.

One young black bear was out on a half-sunken log that protruded from a green mass of marsh grass. I watched him rake his paw through the water and presumed he was fishing for frogs. It would have made an interesting photograph but his dark fur blended with the shadows behind him. The sun, too, had slipped below the lip of the encircling range leaving him and half the lake in blue shadows.

At my approach the bear scarcely paused to glance my way, turned deftly on his log then shuffled down its length to lose himself in the gloom beneath the trees on the shore.

The afternoon was wearing away. I decided to make for the island where I would camp the night. Crossing a small bay there was the unmistakable 'V' of rippled wavelets left in the wake of a brown head.

I rowed hard to overtake the swimmer. At twenty yards he sounded the alarm with an abrupt smack of his broad tail. A moment later he emerged again, circled the boat, sounded, then dived again. This performance was repeated several times. By guessing roughly where he would come up the next time and keeping the camera continually at the ready I managed to photograph him the instant he made the water explode into spray with his tail. It was a unique shot and one I shall always associate with the echo and re-echo of his report bouncing from hillside to mountain cliff and back again across the quiet of that soft evening.

Finally he tired of circling me and left for good. In the twilight of the north I beached the boat on a rock shelf that jutted from the island. A few feet below the surface was a white sand beach, now submerged by the spring flood waters, but no doubt an entrancing spot in late summer at lower levels.

Soon a fire crackled and talked to me from its bed between three stones. Out on the lake a pair of loons talked to each other about this intruder. Few sounds can convey that poignant mood of the north-lands' utter solitude that is borne by a loon's weird wail; especially if it comes wavering through the semi-darkness splitting the twilight with melancholy notes.

Somehow it is a sound that with familiarity fascinates me. There are a pair of Pacific loons which winter at the river mouth in front of my house. Even in the midnight hours I can hear their cry, yet in the sound there is deep comfort for they are noble birds.

With descending darkness the loons moved down the lake. Silence draped itself across the valley as the last glow of light died above the highest ridge.

I hugged the embers of the fire. This had been a rewarding day! With deep contentment of heart I relived its tranquil hours and knew they had made me a richer man in mind and body.

Just then the long wavering howl of a timber wolf reached me from a ridge to the east. There the faint aura of a rising moon silhouetted the timber on the skyline like a series of sharp saw teeth.

Again there was the howl, this time joined by others. The primitive sound had a way of bouncing against the rocks and trees before striking my ear and I wondered exactly where it came from.

The wolves were on the move. They were hunting, and I sensed from the sound that their quarry was seeking the safety of the lake.

The last call I heard came from the shoreline. After that there was only a long-drawn silence: A gentle murmur of water lapping the rocks whenever a breeze caressed the lake; then dreamland.

143

At dawn it was a wolf call that awoke me. This time it came from the opposite side of the lake. I guessed that the deer or moose they had followed swam across in the darkness and they had encircled the lake during the night to pick up the trail.

Hurriedly I threw on my jacket and walked to the end of the island. Sunrise silvered the water and there, breaking the mirror, was a big cow moose swimming strongly. What a magnificent bit of grim drama was being enacted here.

Deeply moved I watched her make the shallows. She was heavy in calf. Twice she had outwitted the wolves. The last trailing cry sounded from the hill and it betrayed the disappointment of the hunt. When forest swallowed her dark bulk I felt a wave of admiration sweep through my being. What a splendid creature to preserve both her unborn offspring, and herself.

She was headed again for the hills from which the wolves had driven her. I knew, too, that if I was to secure moose pictures it would have to be on higher ground. The lake had been rich with life, but it was no place to linger now looking for these grand beasts.

Breakfast was eaten, my pack loaded, the fire out, and the camp ground cleaned and tidy. For a few minutes I loitered, drinking in the deep stillness of this spot. Perhaps I would never pass this way again. On my mind a fine etching could be made by a few quiet moments of reflection.

Engrossed thus I was startled by the unexpected appearance of the two loons gliding around the headland, a stone's toss away. Before they spotted me and deployed I had secured a tranquil picture. Their black and white plumage against this green world of theirs composed a colour photograph which I can never view without a profound sense of well-being and utter happiness creeping into my bones.

Satisfied beyond measure I launched the boat; rowed back to my starting point; cached it as carefully as I had found it; then took up my pack. One backward glance through the trees showed a sliver of sun-washed water. On it there drifted two tiny specks.

In serene solitude were left the loons and the lake.

18
The Curious Caribou

I HAVE entitled this chapter 'The Curious Caribou' for two main reasons. First, because this species has been described by many outdoorsmen as the most inquisitive creature of our wilds. As it so happens I have seldom found them to be anything but wary. The second reason being that the caribou is in itself a most unusual and interesting animal.

There would be no object in my attempting to lead the reader to believe that the caribou with which I am familiar is the barren ground caribou of the far north. Rather those which I have followed and photographed are our mountain caribou which seldom are found in the great massed herds that were once common in the northern type.

The caribou is a typical example of a species which, like our North American bison, once numbered in hundreds of thousands. They were naïvely considered an almost inexhaustible natural resource to which little thought or care was given for preservation. Today we suddenly find ourselves confronted with the very sobering shaking reality that the caribou herds are dwindling at an alarming rate, especially west of the Mackenzie River. Those to the east, for some reason not yet determined, appear to hold their own. This decline has been serious enough to threaten the survival of some Indian tribes in the north who depend upon them for their sustenance and survival.[1]

Various causes for the disappearance of the caribou have been advanced. Increased predation by wolves, increased hunting with high-powered weapons, disease of unknown origin, and an increasingly impoverished range have all been suggested as contributors to the decimation of caribou ranks.

Biologists are now studying the animals in an attempt to find the main root of their dilemma. Their findings may in fact uncover a combination of evils rather than any single source of trouble.

What has happened to the barren ground caribou has, in a similar though far less spectacular manner, been going on with our mountain species. Little importance or publicity has been attached to the steady disappearance of this creature from its former haunts. True enough big-game hunters and guides shake their heads gloomily when recalling the 'old days' when fine bands of caribou could be found on many of the upland meadows, where today they are not seen.

One summer I spent a week in country which formerly was a caribou paradise: A country of high alpine fields covering hundreds of square miles with such picturesque place names as 'Bull Valley' and 'Caribou Meadows'—titles earned by the fine herds found there in years gone by. During that entire week I failed to see a single caribou.

---

[1] Reports which have just reached me since this chapter was originally written, indicate that caribou ranks are once more beginning to swell. I have no personal evidence of this; if, indeed, it is true, no one will be more delighted than I.

Yet less than twenty years ago a herd of 100 head was not an uncommon sight in this wild bit of country.

To me this is a loss which we cannot afford in our wilderness wildlife. In a nation as enlightened as Canada we should spare no effort to guarantee that this major big-game species is given every chance to stage a comeback. In my humble opinion the mountain caribou deserves scientific investigation, for it cannot hope to survive on numbers alone as its northern cousin may do.

Taken collectively a bunch of caribou fail to impress one perhaps as would a herd of haughty elk. They do not carry the feeling of might inherent in moose. They lack the rugged splendour of wild sheep, or the bold daring of the mountain goat. Even the light gracefulness of common deer is absent. Still they possess an elusive charm of their own.

Somehow I believe this attraction is closely bound up with the remote country they live in; with their ability to withstand rigorous winter conditions that would make an elk or moose whimper for relief. Part of their winsomeness too may lie in their retiring habits, their shyness and timidity.

Whatever the reason, this much I do know, that few times in my wide experiences of the wilds have I ever been quite as deeply moved by a first view of any animal as the morning I laid eyes on my first caribou bull in his breeding prime.

Repeated failures to find caribou had whetted my determination all the more to photograph them. I had made at least three mountain trips in the hope of encountering caribou and every one, though rewarding in other wildlife, drew a blank with these animals. Oh, I had seen their tracks, great round 'horseshoe-like' tracks quite unlike the hoofmarks of any other animals, in the shore mud of lakes, in the soft ground of upland meadows. I had come across their beds fresh, and sometimes even warm, where they laid in the dampness of deep forests. Their dung had been on the trail twenty-six times, but never did I see the owner, even though he may have passed that way only seven minutes earlier.

Then one morning in the northern Canadian Rockies my luck changed. Men had deserted the mountains for the valleys, warm houses, and the shelter of the trees. I was alone up on the snow-covered slopes, alone with my hopes of finding caribou.

147

A blizzard had blanketed the hills in the night. In the dimness of an autumn dawn I started out on my quest, chilled to the white marrow of my bones before I had gone a mile. Then I came to a slope where the night's howling wind had brushed the snow from the ground into the valley below. It left tufts of black moss and lichens poking up like burned nuts sticking to the white icing of a cake. Here the caribou had come to feed in the dawn and their tracks betrayed them.

It took a few minutes to unravel the twisted trails. They overlapped and crisscrossed every way. Caribou are restless roamers and always on the move. Soon I determined the general direction of their movement and set off cautiously. A few hundred yards away I spotted a bunch in a grove of dwarfed, wind-stunted trees. With them was a bull at his best. The white flowing cape or 'apron' surmounting his dark thick body made him a splendid sight. I was glad I had come. I began to feel warm too—warm with the exciting prospects of photographing him.

I stood perfectly still, going on the assumption that these notoriously 'curious' creatures would wonder what I was and come closer to investigate. What an empty hope that was! Instead they gave me a brief once-over, wheeled and fled with a plume of fine snow flying up from behind their paddle-like feet.

What I had to learn before the day died was that, if alarmed, these animals will travel tirelessly for many miles before settling down again. By dark I had secured several photographs, but purely through sheer perseverance in ploughing behind them through the snow hour after hour. That night I was barely able to make camp again so weary were my legs from the punishment of the trail.

Where I would break through the wind-polished crust of the snow and flounder to my knees, the caribou with their round snow-shoe like feet had travelled swiftly over the top. I have been told that they make use of this same advantage in crossing thin ice on lakes. They appear to possess an uncanny knack of determining exactly how thick the ice is and whether it will bear their weight.

Odd as it may seem, caribou are a species of conflicting characteristics. They are often spoken of as 'soft' animals. By this it is meant that they are timid, docile creatures, who live in fear of wolves and cougars. It has been suggested that this timidity, especially at the critical time when the young are born, will cause them to reject their offspring and flee in terror, rather than stand and fight as elk, moose, or even deer will do. If this is true it would be easy to understand why they could not maintain their numbers in the face of a rising wolf population.

But the term 'soft' is equally applicable to their favourite feed. In the spring and summer they prefer the soft lush grasses and herbage found in damp places. In the fall after freeze up they turn to mosses and lichens. First they use the low growing forms found on the open rocks, but which must first be softened by rain and snow to suit their tastes. Later when deep snow makes these unattainable they turn to the mosses and lichens which hang from trees or cling to high rocks.

On the other hand caribou are hardy and able to subsist under the most rigorous winter conditions. The greatest single provision for this is without question their remarkable coat of hair. Not only is it thick but also unusually efficient as an insulating cover. This is because each hair is hollow and this air space within the hairs themselves gives added protection against frigid temperatures.

The same principle applies to wading and swimming in ice-cold water. The coat of hollow hair holds them well up out of the water with its buoyancy and still insulates them against its penetration. A brisk shake frees the body of moisture in a silver spray, leaving the animals virtually dry.

Some authorities believe that the caribou is declining because their range is being usurped in places by the moose and elk. This I question seriously. The moose is a bottom-dwelling animal, favouring the forests, marshes, burns, and willow thickets. Occasionally a wandering bull will invade the caribou's high country, but in the main there is little conflict.

Where elk have been introduced there may indeed be competition for summer range. But the winter period, which is the critical one, finds elk far away at lower levels whereas the caribou stick it out on the hill-tops.

A theory commonly held in many quarters is that a substantial increase in wolf numbers during recent years has worked havoc with the caribou herds. This is open to question. Wolves are tremendous travellers. They range far and wide. To obtain anything like an accurate census on them presents a formidable task.

149

Because the subject of wolf predation is at present such a controversial one all across Canada, I have refrained purposely from elaborating on the species in this book. I have listened to their howl in the forest at night. I have followed their tracks along the mud of lakeshores and through the snow. But in all my travels in the bush only once have I ever encountered a band of these creatures in daylight, and that was when a group of four attempted to kill a young bull elk they had surrounded at a great distance from me. I have come across their kills in various places but just the same I do not wish to take sides for or against them. Along with all other wild creatures they have their part to play in nature's scheme of things. Perhaps a few years hence we will understand their role better than we do at this present moment of confusion.

As for the caribou cows who sometimes look grotesque with their ill-shaped horns, they appear to make little use of these appendages in fending off wolves. This is all the more astonishing when one stops to realize that they are the only members of the deer family in which the females possess horns and which might conceivably put up some stiff resistance to predators' attacks. Nor are the bulls impressive with their drooping demeanour until the fall rut begins. What they may have lacked until then, however, they certainly make up for in the glory of their breeding regalia. At this time the males are elegant specimens which cannot help but arouse the enthusiasm of any lover of the wilds.

In my mind I prefer to picture them that way. Then, when the winter sends its storms across the heights, I like to think of these hardy ones defying its frigid wrath and surviving in their gentle humble way where other more spectacular animals would perish.

Eventually there came a day when all the dreams, the hopes, the desperate desire to be in close contact with caribou condensed themselves into real blood and bone on the high wind-blown alplands cradled by the crags of the continental divide. It had taken five years of persistent searching, climbing, and packing—then suddenly the rich rewards were in my lap—like a medal fondled in the hands of an athlete who has strained his heart to win it.

It was mid-August; hot with haze; the skies and mountain valleys canopied with a dim pall of blue wood smoke that drifted in high overhead on the flow of western air. The gigantic summer forest fires of British Columbia pushed their loaded clouds of pungent smoke and cinders into an already burning sky that carried them steadily towards the Rockies.

I laboured up the trail under a pack made cumbersome by the close warm air; the clinging flies that relished the warmth; and mosquitoes that droned in hordes. A man with a vision can endure great hardships. That evening I clung desperately to the tattered reports of a band of mountain caribou that had been sighted in McArib Pass. If they were there I was determined to find them.

As darkness flowed into the valley I ascended, I caught a glimpse of shining snowfields and open meadows above me. Caribou country! Weary muscles found fresh vigour in the view. Hurriedly, almost carelessly, I pushed on, crossing and recrossing the stream that found birth on the high fields of ice and snow.

I found still another log fallen across the stream to serve as a bridge. Gingerly I edged along it—then it gave way and the next instant I was back down, pack under water, floundering beneath the log where the current's force pushed me relentlessly.

By a miracle I managed to hold my camera above my head with one arm while I fought to free my soaked body from its predicament with the other. Ice-charged water can be cool indeed at 6,000 feet, and especially when night is near under a clear sky.

It did not take me long to start a mighty fire. All around the dancing flame I draped my saturated gear—including a sleeping-bag that would steam ominously for hours while its filling dried ever so reluctantly. Meanwhile I danced about the warmth like a naked dervish, driving heat and warmth back into the marrow of my bones.

That night I dreamed of caribou: herds of caribou—moving across these mountain ranges. If only it would come true!

Dawn found me above timberline and into their realm.

Again and again in this book I have mentioned being moved by mountain grandeur—but this was an interlude apart from and transcending anything I had ever seen. I have climbed, rambled, and explored in the Olympics, the Coast Range, the Cascades, the Caribou Mountains, the Selkirks, the Monashees, the Sierras, and other sections of the Rockies, but for sheer, magnetic grandeur this panorama before me was unmatched.

151

Imagine, if you can, for but a moment, coming up over a snow-dappled saddle at over 7,000 feet. The sun red in its rising is behind your back tinting the broken rock of Oldhorn mountain with rich rouge. A pink glow lies over the snow and ice that lingers in patches between fields of shattered shale. Away to the west sweep mile upon unmeasured mile of open green grassland, alpine meadows that start at your feet and stretch to the dim horizon of tangled blue peaks in British Columbia. Here a splash of fireweed bursts into brilliant bloom against blue sky; there a carpet of paint-brush glows against a snowfield. Then back and against all this place those majestic crags of the Ramparts that thrust their splendid rugged crowns into the heavens.

This was the world in which I was to find and photograph my caribou: a realm so utterly overpowering that for the first time in my life I felt incapable of photographing its splendour. In fact it presented an artistic challenge which I am sure could be met only by men of the very highest and most profound sensitivity.

But I was after caribou. The mountains would be waiting there when I came back another time—as come I surely would—but the caribou may well have moved away. So I started in to glass the heights.

About mid-morning I picked up some pepper-like specks on a distant snowfield. They were almost indistinguishable from the broken rocks, but my quest was fulfilled—caribou! At least three miles of scree, glacial drift, and snow separated us. I started the stalk.

So determined was I to succeed that I took off my boots and actually stalked the last 300 yards in stocking feet for absolute silence. There were two cows, two calves, and a young bull on the snow; the rest relaxed on the rocks.

The eternal persecution endured by these animals from the large flies surpassed anything I had ever seen before. I had just taken a picture of the bull at fifty feet, when unable to stand the insects any longer he rushed off down the slope in a frenzy. Hour after hour, day upon day, I followed, watched, and very nearly wept for these creatures as they moved from snowfield to snowfield seeking relief from their tormentors. The cows with calves and younger bulls appeared to suffer most. Some were so thin I could count their ribs with ease. They had simply run off all their flesh.

That first night I camped where I could watch a small band of black dots on the greensward. Enfolding them up here on top of the world were peaks of red, ochre, grey, and black that changed hues with the setting sun. Utter solitude—utter serenity.

The next day I explored a different basin and there discovered a band of no less than fifty-nine animals. There were prime bulls still in the velvet but starting to grow their regal mane and cape, and there were young calves only a few weeks old.

The longer I spent with them the more intrigued I was with the erratic behaviour of the species. For no good reason that I could see a cow would suddenly start to gallop away down a slope all on her own, leaving behind a small calf with utter indifference. The calves in turn seemed undisturbed by the sudden disappearance of their mother who in some cases, I noticed, had not returned after several hours.

Two bulls would be lying side by side. One would leap to his feet, start to run, or more properly trot, as they do in their peculiar gait, and run for several miles. The other bull meanwhile drowsily continued to chew his cud.

They seemed inordinately fond of licking certain mineral earths. One spot in particular this had been done so relentlessly that an acre or more of ground was completely bare.

For animals who spend so much of their time standing or walking in soft snow, I was amazed to see the ease with which they traversed the scree, broken rock, and slate where even I had great difficulty in travelling with tough boots. Their hooves must be of marvellous material to stand such treatment without cracking, splitting, or laming the animals.

I watched one band of twenty-five actually run up a snow slope which must have approached seventy degrees. It was so steep I could not climb it on hands and feet without cutting steps. Yet they moved both up and down this impossible face with casual abandon.

Another afternoon a cow and calf that I startled fled up a rock cliff where I am confident only mountain sheep or goats could possibly climb.

Apart from when they are actually on snow, I know of no other big-game species that blends so completely with their background of broken rock. To spot them in such surroundings requires the keenest eyesight. One colour photograph I took has twenty-nine caribou on a rock slope. Unless a stranger is told that there are animals in the picture they are never noticed.

My greatest difficulty with these herds was the simple problem of trying to get close enough for good pictures—especially of big bulls. They showed none of the curiosity which has been a hallmark of the species. At sight or scent of me they fled every time. I tried every trick in the bag to arouse this instinct, but without success.

Finally one day my determination to photograph a fine bull was to be rewarded—I thought. At dawn I discovered one young bull and a noble old companion working their way slowly up a meadow towards the snow. The wind and sun were not in my favour and for five hours I crept, crawled, and climbed along behind them.

By dint of cautious manoeuvring I managed to surprise the pair on a snow patch and secured a rather spectacular shot of them against a backdrop of open meadowland with blue mountains beyond. This was the only favour the young bull would grant me. A few seconds later he broke into a trot and was gone forever over the farthest horizon.

In a way I was elated to have only one animal left to stalk—particularly since he was the best bull I had ever seen. For two more hours I followed his erratic movements of grazing, running, grazing, trotting.

I had been on his trail now for the better part of seven hours, never able to get much closer than about a hundred yards. By great good luck he moved into a small hollow giving me a chance to creep up on him. This was a tremendous break since cover, apart from a stray rock here and there, was non-existent.

To my astonishment I was able to squirm, wriggle, and belly crawl through the heather until he came into focus at sixty feet. My excitement ran so high I felt the camera tremble in my sweaty palms. I took two pictures, then felt the film at the end of its roll. What luck!

Feverishly I lay there prone, trying to reload. My motions caught his eye. In an instant he was alert, poised in all his glory.

Gingerly he started to step towards me. I lay stupefied with an empty camera in my hand. He came on until not more than twenty-five to thirty feet separated us.

With a snort he wheeled and spun away.

Those curious caribou!

155

19
Winter Weather

PHOTOGRAPHING wild animals in winter weather poses a challenge involving difficulties and hardships not at first apparent to anyone who has never tried it.

The other morning I was out in the mountains stalking a small band of California Bighorn sheep. The temperature was around zero with a mean wind gusting from the north. After a grim scramble up a rugged icy peak in pursuit of my quarry, I finally reached the summit with an inner glow of sweet satisfaction.

This turned to bitter disgust when I attempted to focus the rangefinder of the camera on the sheep and found that it was frozen solid. The instrument had been sent to the manufacturers for a complete overhaul only a few months before. Evidently a drop or two of excess oil had been left on the precision parts of the rangefinder. During the long three-hour stalk in the cold the lubricant had thickened and congealed until it was impossible to adjust the focusing device at all. I was forced then to guess the distance at which the animals stood posed before me in all their grandeur, hoping that my judgment might be somewhere near correct.

It only added to my chagrin to discover that the camera functioned beautifully again after being returned to the warmth for half an hour. Of course, one could carry it under his clothing close to the body at all times, but like a rifle or any other weapon used in the hunt, it needs to be ever at the ready for instant use. If not, opportunities can be missed which will never be repeated. Animals seldom pause or pose long enough for the unprepared photographer to arrange his equipment.

The other day was a case in point. The band of sheep had ascended the rocky peak by way of a knife ridge. Leaving this they spiralled around the summit going with the wind. Knowing that I would have a better opportunity to meet them unexpectedly, I circled from the ridge in the opposite direction around the mountain.

Naturally I was intent on the Bighorns. I was fully occupied, too, with negotiating the rocks that had become sheathed in treacherous ice, now innocently covered with a fresh mantle of new snow. I would be lucky indeed to get off the heights in one piece without broken bones.

Suddenly I peered over the lip of a great rock slab. There, framed in wild majesty by a stunted pine, stood three mule deer taking the sun in a small snow basin below me.

It was a superb setting which lasted only momentarily, but the camera was ready and I got the picture. The wary animals had detected my footsteps above them and waited only an instant to watch my head appear before bounding away. Now if I had had to fuss and fume with getting my camera out from beneath my jacket, the chance would have been lost for ever.

One encounters some other obstacles, too, that would not at first be apparent. At certain temperatures and levels of atmospheric humidity every breath of air that is exhaled from the lungs envelops one in a miniature cloud of steam. If one is still and attempting to remain unnoticed this friendly little wraith of vapour swirling about the head is bound to betray one's presence to any wild creatures on the alert. My method of trying to reduce this to a minimum is to tie a woollen scarf around my face so that the vapour is at least dissipated somewhat in passing through the woven material.

I am frequently asked what I consider to be the most important ingredient in stalking game, to which the answer is always 'the ability to freeze'. Sometimes people think I use the word 'freeze' in the literal sense. Normally I do not; for this is a term commonly used in describing the art of remaining motionless for long periods of time while being watched by wary animals. On occasion one has to do this in the most exhausting positions—such as poised on one leg in mid-stride, crouched in a cramped position or perchance flat with your face buried in the snow or tormented by some irritating insects.

In winter work, however, 'freezing' can in truth become a very literal experience and at the same time very painful. When temperatures are low only the constant activity of the muscles will maintain one in comparative comfort. As soon as the body is motionless cold begins to penetrate the extremities of fingers, face, and feet with excruciating results.

For myself in particular this is a painfully rapid process. Years of malaria, combined with poor blood circulation, soon leave my hands and toes curled and cramped like members formed of chilled cast iron. Nor does feeling or life return without vigorous rubbing, stamping, and exercise. In fact one day in the Rockies I feared I had passed the point of no return, because it took nearly twelve hours to restore the use of my hands.

Gloves are cumbersome to manipulate a camera with, mitts are even worse. In order to insure that the camera will be held perfectly steady and the shutter properly released, I generally remove my gloves. The cold does not delay in taking advantage of this exposed flesh. Consequently the picture has to be shot quickly and accurately with no time wasted.

Another unexpected phenomena which can prove exasperating to the winter photographer is snow fog. With atmospheric conditions at

159

the precise point necessary for its formation, a dense ground-hugging fog will develop over snow that may persist for several days. Sometimes it will fluctuate, returning periodically throughout the daylight hours and dissipating at night, thus adding insult to injury.

Possibly the toughest winter trip I ever made was complicated by fog and almost proved my undoing. In fact never before had I encountered this phenomena and the experience is well worth telling.

Early winter had laid a blanket of snow almost ten inches deep over the high alpine meadows and timber ridges lying between Battle and Trophy mountains in British Columbia. This was caribou country and

I was keen to film them in a winter setting. Only once before had I been into this territory, and because of its remarkable beauty felt drawn there again.

It was about noon when I set out alone with my pack, starting from the thickly overgrown river bottoms drenched with the dripping wetness of half rain, half snow that clung to the vegetation.

This was cut-over country that had grown up with a thick tangle of young willow, alder, and aspens. Because of the abundant browse there were numerous moose and mule deer in the area. As I climbed the switchback trail I could see a dense layer of cloud settling down over the ridges. I dismissed the view from my mind as nothing more than the usual cloud formation of the high country.

Soon there began to be snow on the trail and cold snow droplets clinging to all the foliage along the path. It was beginning to drench my clothing as I brushed against it, so I picked up a bit of root to beat the bushes as I climbed.

It was not long until gloom and darkness settled around me and I had the sensation of ascending into a pall of cold grey fog in which I could see only a few yards ahead.

Suddenly out of this enfolding shroud I heard the ominous sounds of a bull moose grunting his challenge and coming rapidly towards me. He had picked up the sounds of my beating the bush along the trail and must have thought I was a rival bull slashing with his antlers.

The thick fog, for that was what I was in, had muffled the sound of his approach and before I could get the pack off my back and seize the camera he was challenging me from a distance of some thirty feet— still unseen.

I quickly sized up my position and decided to try and entice him to come a little closer so that I could capture the mood of his craggy form looming out of the fog. He seemed unsure of what I was and my continued beating on the bush would not budge him from the thicket to which he clung.

There were no trees of any size about which I could climb except one small pine about twelve feet high. I scrambled up this in an effort to get a view over the top of the dense brush. To my delight I caught a glimpse of him standing in full view for just a split second as the fog parted, then it closed over him again. He was an immense beast and

161

far away the largest bull moose I had ever seen. The stray eddy of air that parted the fog must have carried my scent to him, for he plunged off up the trail with snorts of defiance and apprehension.

It was a bitter pill to swallow not getting a picture, but I was determined to try again so I shouldered the pack and headed up after him. The next hour or so was one of the weirdest wildlife episodes of my mountain forays. The fog rolled and swirled around the slopes in smoke-like masses. Out of these gloomy folds the bulk of the massive black bull would emerge for just a moment then melt away into the gloom. Again and again I would be just on the verge of pressing the shutter when a solid grey wall would come between and the ghost-like form was gone. It was tantalizing the way he stuck to the trail ahead of me until finally the dense timber at the edge of the cut-over country wrapped its darker shadows around him and he was gone for good.

Where before the trail, even though under deep snow, had been reasonably easy to follow in the bush, it was now swallowed by the timber and became almost impossible to trace. It was a trail that had been little used, numerous blow downs blocked it, the old blazes had weathered until they were scarcely discernible, while in many places driving snow clinging to the trunks obliterated them entirely.

Before long I realized that to reach the shelter at the summit before night would be a nip and tuck affair. The fog hovered in the trees and my progress on the trail was slowed to a mere crawl. I would put down the pack, prowl ahead to find the path from one blaze to another over the tangle of down timber, then return to pick up the pack and gain a few more yards.

This was exhausting sort of progress. My outer clothing was drenched from the wet snow through which I floundered, and perspiration from the tremendous exertion soaked my underclothes.

The higher I climbed the colder it became and to pause for more than merely a few minutes was to invite a serious chill. Darkness was just closing in to add its weight of gloom to the shrouds of fog through which I crept when all of a sudden I broke from the timber-line into the open meadows of the alpine country. Almost as quickly I detected the twinkle of an early star through the overcast above me. In a few moments I found myself in open glades that bore familiar landmarks from my previous trip here.

163

Somehow a keen exhilaration of triumph flooded over me, for I had pushed on in spite of misgivings and frequent temptations to turn back down the mountain. I had conquered my own fear.

Weary to the point of utter exhaustion from ploughing through the soft wet snow, I had to stop and rest almost every hundred yards. Finally the cabin loomed up out of the spruce tree shadows. I stumbled to its door and dumped the pack on the deep drift of snow piled on its porch.

Fortunately for me the last occupant of this cabin had been an outdoorsman of the 'old school'. There by the stove lay a pile of fine dry split kindling, several feathered sticks too had been whittled ready to take a match, while armfuls of dry wood were stacked against the wall.

So exhausted and cold was I from the long climb that to have had to gather fuel for a fire might well have proved the last spark that would have blinked out from my defiant spirit on that wild winter mountain.

While I lay on the bunk listening to the crackling fire I recalled how low the flame of life had burned in my companion in this very selfsame cabin the last time I camped there. Then it was through the long night hours I had watched him fight for his recovery.

Perhaps that was why sleep came so deep and delicious that night. The slumber of contentment after a battle of muscle and will against snow and fog and fear.

At dawn I was up and met the sunrise. It was gold and glass clear. With its arrival under blue skies I was treated to a golden day on the height. Gone was the fog, the greyness, the cloud.

But they were there again the next morning.

Regretfully I shouldered the pack and crept back down the mountain slipping and sliding along my old tracks which alone guided me through the gloom.

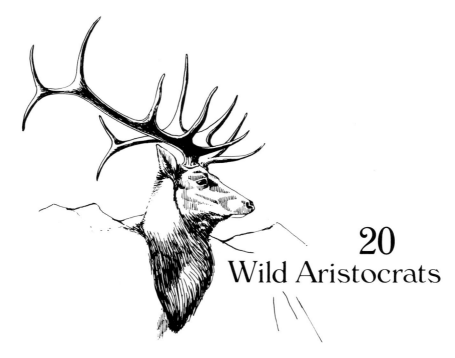

20
Wild Aristocrats

THIS morning I was in the city on business. While sitting in the office waiting for my appointment I was thrilled to see, hanging on the wall, a magnificent print of a bull elk. The picture, although reproduced from a painting which has become the world renowned hallmark of this particular firm, might well have been a photograph. For just a few precious minutes I lived again in the high misty mountains that formed the background to the majestic bull in his prime. Somehow the clatter of the typewriters, the stuffy, tobacco-smoked room, the tight constricting pressure of the city were dissolved around me. Again I felt the dampness of clouds against my cheeks; the droplets of silver mist were in my hair; the clean cool air of the peaks filled my lungs; then across the chasm of time I heard the monarch's ringing bugle fill the valleys of my memory with fresh vigour.

Then the door opened, and I was called back to the present. But that is what elk have always done to me. There is about this species a dignity and charm difficult to define. For that reason I have called them the 'Wild Aristocrats'.

The mountain goat has never failed to fascinate me with his hardy ways and nimble exploits. I have always been fond of the Rocky Mountain Big Horn with his cunning and his strength. The ponderous moose is not without his own massive impressiveness. Bears of all kinds are always interesting; while the deer possess a dainty winsomeness of rare grace.

But when it comes to elk I seem to have a special warm niche reserved for them in my heart. This can be best explained, I believe, because they combine many of the best qualities to be found in all the others. Because they are essentially a migratory animal that moves from the lowlands in winter to the highest meadows in summer they are hardy adaptable creatures accustomed to a wide range of environments. I have watched them feeding in the foggy rain-drenched forests thick with sallal and 'devil's club' on the coast. I have also photographed them high on the snow-crusted shoulders of the Rockies.

In country where human beings are seldom seen they are wary creatures who demand the highest degree of stalking. Nor can one ever hope to see a more excellent sight than a proud herd bull with his harem, challenging all the 'outriders' to combat. To my mind the bull elk in breeding prime is a spectacle of regal splendour.

Because of their size, elk convey a feeling of strength and might not associated with deer. At the same time they have an agility and proud carriage that is wonderful to watch. When the antler tips glint white in the sun then there is added the ultimate touch of dignity.

All of these qualities, combined in a species whose habits are so interesting, naturally inspired me to attempt photographing them in their upland haunts. It is not surprising that I should make the first attempt close to home in the Olympic Mountains.

Oddly enough this is one species, out of the many I have photographed, that gave me happy results on the first try. 'Beginners' luck' applied in this instance even if it never has in any other animal pursuits. Usually my best pictures have only been taken after days, weeks, months, or in some cases even years of repeated effort.

It was July of an unusually hot dry summer on the Pacific coast. I decided a brief trip into the Olympics would be blessed with fair weather, for the skies were a brassy blue canopy day after day.

167

Consulting with the game wardens of the region my hopes were not lifted with the news that few elk had been sighted in recent weeks. Because of the heat it was supposed that the herds were sheltering in dense timber. A poor place indeed either to try and find them at all or to photograph them. It was suggested that my best prospects for success would be to reconnoitre the mountains from a chartered aircraft; then, knowing where the herds were, locating them on foot would be less difficult.

A stubborn streak runs through my makeup. If I was going to hunt elk it would be the hard way. At least what I felt was the only true sporting way—on foot. In any case I had no funds for flying around with.

Going on one of my 'hunches' I threw my pack on my back and headed into the hills for a basin where I had once seen elk years before. That time I was merely hiking, not camera hunting as on this trip. The memory of that other first evening was alive in my mind as I plodded up the trail under a heavy pack, made much heavier by the heat and mosquitoes of this hot July afternoon.

I could remember how on the first occasion I walked this trail it was early September and the blueberries were full and lush and sweet. My chum and I gorged on them as we chattered our way up. Carelessly we broke from the brush above timber line and startled a herd of elk in a little green glen. With snorts of apprehension they rushed up the slopes in the dusk and vanished over a ridge on which we camped that evening.

The entire night was enlivened with the bugling of the bulls in the valley below us. I cannot recall a more enchanting night under the stars than that one, and I have spent a good many out in the wild places in my sleeping-bag.

So as I sweated up the slopes alone this time, stopping to drink deeply from the coolness of every rivulet I crossed, there burned deep within me a faith that again I would find elk in this magic spot. I slipped from the thick growth above timberline—this time with the utmost caution—into the green glade.

It was empty!

Then I swept my eyes over the high patches of snow that stuck to the steep slopes towering ahead. Two tiny dark specks, like mere pepper grains, attracted my attention. I put the binoculars on them. Two bull elk were lying on the snow.

It was late afternoon by now and I felt a stalk should not be planned until the next day. Soon the sun would drop behind the ridges and I would have to work in the shadows during what few hours of sunlight remained. Accordingly I pushed on to the old cherished camp-site on the ridge and made an early supper. If not molested I was sure the bulls would linger on the slope until the next day. Then I would have the double advantages of being fresh, with a rising sun behind my back.

With supper over I strolled casually along the ridge through the twilight to see if there might be game tracks on the snow patches or around the marshy edges of the alpine fields. These fields formed a belt of open meadowland along the crest of the ridge, flanked on either side by dense spruce forest.

I found not a solitary hoofprint. However, I reassured myself that the two bulls would provide all the material I needed the next day. In the meantime I revelled in the grandeur and immensity of the mountain massifs that surrounded me on every side. The glow of sunset painted them pink and purple with a beauty I cannot hope to convey on this paper, nor even on film.

Retracing my footsteps in the twilight I was suddenly startled by the unexpected appearance of a whole herd of elk boiling up out of the trees at the edge of the meadow. It was one of the strangest sensations! One moment nothing in sight except green grass, nodding lupins, and glimmering snow. The next instant a milling mass of cows, calves, and bulls spilling out on to the sward from the shadows of the spruce trees.

Their arrival was so utterly surprising that I scarcely had time to drop down on all fours and crouch behind some stunted shrubs. Before I realized what was happening the hungry cows, eager for the new herbage that had not been touched yet that summer, were swarming around and past me.

One young cow and her calf were barely thirteen yards from me when she caught the human scent. The warning blast of air from her nostrils threw the whole herd to attention. Cows called their whimpering, fuzzy-coated calves, and the bulls searched for danger on the wind with their nostrils.

The cow nearest to me did not flee but stood staring at my huddled form, snorting with mingled alarm and defiance. I took several photographs, but the light was so weak the film could not hope to capture the

169

ELK CALF, TWO HOURS OLD

ASPENS GNAWED BY ELK

scene. One does those things anyway, hoping against hope that perhaps a miracle will happen and the results might just turn out better than they do.

By now the cows, curious to see what caused the alarm, came up and encircled me. It was like a circus ring in reverse with the human being the centre of interest. A frisking breeze confirmed my identity and the lot panicked. They turned and fled up the meadow like a bunch of cattle on a pasture. The bulls brought up the rear together with a few dry cows.

I stood up from my cramped crouch. Into the dark faded the muted sounds of hooves on sod, punctuated by the 'eeu-eeu-eeu' of the calves crying for their mothers to wait for them.

Excited yet contented I made for camp. What a stroke of good fortune! Tomorrow would be a tremendous day!

Whether it was the excitement or whether it was actually that hot I cannot say for sure, but that night at over 7,000 feet I slept on top of my sleeping-bag rather than inside it. Actually I got very little sleep. How could one with such a day in store?

By four-thirty the next morning I had breakfasted and broken camp. I did not dare to light a fire lest the smoke drift to the elk, and I was determined no pains should be spared to disturb them as little as possible. With the first dawn light I scanned the snow slopes for the two bulls. They had gone! My heart sank. Then suddenly I discovered them again with a third companion feeding in dense brush below the snowfields. It would be a difficult stalk across the open face of the slope.

The first part was not as difficult as I had imagined. There was sufficient dead ground that I was able to travel quite freely across little open glades thickly dotted with wild heathers at the height of their pink bloom.

This gave way to deep rocky gorges and broken bushland. Here was where the bulls were feeding. Climbing to a little promontory I discovered to my dismay that a tremendous steep-walled gulch separated me from the elk. Without being spotted I had worked to the very lip of this cleft in the rock. The three bulls were feeding contentedly on the other side about eighty yards away and I got several pictures of them there.

I was so intent to get a close-up of them that in a rather rash frame of mind I decided to climb down into the gulch and scale the other side. This nearly proved my undoing. It was exceedingly precarious rock work and several times I came close to falling. When, after a tremendous amount of exertion, I did reach the other side it was to

171

look full into the face of a fourth bull, who, while hidden from view all this time, had been intently watching my every move.

With a snort of apprehension he plunged off through a tangle of mountain alders, taking his three companions with him. I was left to get my breath, cool off, and collect my thoughts.

This was just another tantalizing experience that would have to be added to the long list of my photographic disappointments.

The climb out of that basin back to the ridge where I had slept seemed to take hours. A heavy heart has a habit of making heavy feet. To my amazement it was not even twelve noon by the time I regained the ridge. I had a bite to eat and took a cat nap. Such is the great advantage of early starts.

Refreshed, especially with the idea that I still had half a day to take up the trail of the big herd, I pushed off in high spirits again. Just in case they had gone a very long way I tucked extra food in my pouch pocket to last overnight.

It was simple to follow the herd. Their tracks had churned up a distinct trail when they first left me the night before. Later I saw where they settled down to feed. When they got up on bare rock ridges the trail was less obvious and I had to unravel it more carefully.

Eventually I sensed that they were intent on leaving the range on which I had found them and were headed for a deep valley cut off by a knife ridge. To my astonishment they had negotiated this ridge. When I reached its summit and peered over—there they were—a group of brown dots clustered on a snowfield lying way down below me.

Between me and the herd there was virtually no cover. A long bare scree slope of pale yellow sandstone swept down to where the animals rested on the snow. I judged the distance at about 300 yards in a straight line. I guessed that I had about four hours of full sunlight left before the valley would be filled with shadows.

At first the idea of even attempting a stalk across this loose rock in full view the whole time seemed utterly foolish. Two factors though were in my favour. A steady up-draft of air was rising from the valley to carry my scent away. Secondly the sun was directly behind my back, blazing like fury. (I was to curse it for all that before the day was over.)

With tongue in cheek I eased myself over the ridge. I felt utterly naked, somehow, crouched there in full view of the herd. Any second

I was sure they would see me and take their leave. But they did not and this renewed my determination to try an approach. Fortunately I was wearing faded khaki clothes, remnants from African safaris, and these blended beautifully with the pale rock of the slide.

The next four hours are etched so deeply on my mind it is a temptation to recount them here. This would only weary the patient

reader, who unless he himself has ever tackled such a job, cannot appreciate the tense thrilling challenge of such a stalk.

For the better part of four hours I moved forward literally one inch at a time in full view of sixty-four elk. The sun beating on my back plus the strain of controlling every muscle movement made me drip with perspiration. I was so dry my tongue started to swell and I had to suck on a pebble to produce saliva lest I choke. The flies and mosquitoes from which the elk were seeking relief on the snow combined with the heat to make my progress painful. On the other hand as the distance between us shortened and the elk took up more and more space in the viewfinder I realized I was succeeding beyond my wildest dreams.

The cows were restless and would stand up, call their calves, nurse them, feud with one another then return to rest. The bulls, still in the velvet, were inclined to stay to themselves relaxing their heavy antlered heads on the cool snow.

When I was about forty yards away a cow spotted my movement. In an instant the entire herd leaped to their feet and dashed away in unison to a nearby knoll. There they paused briefly to scrutinize me, then rushed off again, down into the next basin.

So parched was my throat that I hurried to the toe of the snowfield to drink from its rivulet of melting water. A few awful mouthfuls nearly made me vomit. It reeked with the manure and urine of the animals that had rested there all day. I spat out the liquid vehemently and started down the stream to find another source. To my utter amazement there I came in full view of the herd again. This time they were all wading and drinking in an emerald blue lake that shimmered under the sun. It entranced me to see calves nursing from their dams while both stood in the water.

This sight of the brown-bodied elk, their rumps golden with sunshine, their dark heads and necks burnished brown against the blue water and green alpine meadows is one I shall ever cherish. A real life dream! What's more, I captured it on film.

When they had finished drinking and frisking the herd moved into another little meadow where I was able to follow and photograph them at very close range before they spotted me. This time a fine bull mounted guard as the cows and calves pounded off into the encircling forest. In wild confusion they crashed through the trees, climbing up the slope that led into the next valley.

Satisfied that the herd was well away the old monarch gave me one last long look; then bounded off in the wake of the surging mass that still trampled its way up through the trees. The crackling, splintering sound of broken limbs was intermingled with the plaintive 'eeu-eeu-eeu' of the wobbly legged calves.

This had been a day of days. A time to remember: an episode to recount again to my children and grandchildren around a flickering camp-fire.

Utterly weary from the long day of tense stalking I went to sit by the little lake. Totally at peace with the world I took off my boots and dangled my feet in the cool water. Twilight enfolded me with long shadowy arms that reached down from the broad shoulders of the hills. The pink-cheeked mountains seemed to smile happily tonight too—for once they had watched me win, first try.

We were all rejoicing.